**ADVANCE PRAISE FOR O**

*Our School* is as beautiful as it is practical; as attentive to the small voices of children as it is to the need for a booming voice of change. Sam takes us where the education reform debate has long needed to go: into the lives of children and teachers, and into the mysterious, exciting, and transformational world of learning. If we listen to him, we can change education. If we don't, we're likely to continue to frustrate our children, our teachers, and ourselves.

—**Timothy P. Shriver**,
chairman and chief executive officer, Special Olympics

*Our School* paints a compulsively readable portrait of two city schools, one public and the other charter, as each strives to build a community of trust and high expectations. By eschewing ideology—instead showing us teaching and learning on the ground—the book delivers a welcome antidote to the ceaseless squabbling that these days passes for policy conversation. It's a must-read for anyone looking for ways to strengthen our schools.

—**David L. Kirp**, author of *Improbable Scholars: The Rebirth of a Great American School System and a Strategy for America's Schools*

Sam Chaltain takes us on an up-close and personal journey into the life of modern American education. Diving into the inner experience of both the classroom and teachers' journeys, our insightful guide teaches us about the dreams and struggles of devoted professionals who wrestle with the challenges of our contemporary educational world to find a way to meet the important needs of a diverse student body. One of the many aspects of this journey that I love is the unique offering for us to experience school life from the inside out, feeling the dreams and aspirations of teachers and how we can creatively re-imagine how students can experience a more creative and empowering process of learning.

—**Daniel J. Siegel**, M.D., clinical professor, UCLA School of Medicine, and author of *Brainstorm: The Power and Purpose of the Teenage Brain*

In this important new book, Sam Chaltain tackles school choice—an issue that has polarized communities across the U.S. Unlike many other books on this topic, Sam does so in a manner that grounds us in the reality of two schools and the lives of the educators and the children they serve. The result is a thoughtful and thought-provoking analysis that will help readers to come away with greater understanding of the complex issues involved in the ongoing conflict between charters and public schools.

—**Pedro Noguera**,
Peter L. Agnew Professor of Education, New York University

Sam Chaltain masterfully illustrates the stories of two schools in the era of open school choice and modern school reform. While these schools are quite different on the shell, Chaltain digs deep, illuminating their shared challenges in creating strong learning environments and opportunities for all of their children, and offering thoughtful recommendations for smarter school policy moving forward.

—**Laura Bornfreund**,
deputy director of early education, New America Foundation

*Our School* is the first book I've read to share the honest human story of our current educational landscape. Sam Chaltain weaves the lives of children and teachers together, along with the larger questions we all face about the future of learning in the U.S. As a result, *Our School* provides the emotional inflection points that are often missing from our growing national debates.

—**Scott Nine**,
executive director, Institute for Democratic Learning in America

In *Our School*, Sam Chaltain uses his voice as an engaged citizen and as a parent to present a profound and eloquent restatement of the mission of public education—to prepare students for active participation in all aspects of a democratic society. As choice among educational services has become a reality for more and more communities, questions of consumer protection and accountability are essential matters for policymakers. For educators, questions of the needs and aspirations of students are crucial. *Our Schools* provides stark illustrations of both perspectives, and the challenges we must address if we are to serve our students and fulfill the mission of America's public schools.

—**Sharon Robinson**,
president and chief executive officer,
American Association of Colleges for Teacher Education

*Our School* is a must-read for educators, parents, and policymakers. Sam Chaltain's astute observations and analysis reinforce what I have advocated for nearly 50 years: that what is in the best interests of children's development and learning must be at the center of all aspects of schooling.

—**James Comer**, M.D.,
Maurice Falk Professor of Child Psychiatry, Yale University

# OUR SCHOOL

## Searching for Community in the Era of Choice

### SAM CHALTAIN

*Foreword by Sir Ken Robinson*

Teachers College
Columbia University
New York and London

Published by Teachers College Press, 1234 Amsterdam Avenue, New York, NY 10027

*Cataloging-in-Publication Data is available from the Library of Congress*

ISBN 978-0-8077-5531-0 (paper)
ISBN 978-0-8077-5559-4 (hardcover)
eISBN 978-0-8077-7288-1

Printed on acid-free paper
Manufactured in the United States of America

21  20  19  18  17  16  15  14          8  7  6  5  4  3  2  1

For Leo and Isaac,

and for all their teachers—past, present, and future.

But how, exactly, will they be reared and educated by us? And does our considering this contribute anything to our goal of discerning that for the sake of which we are considering all these things—in what way justice and injustice come into being in a city.

—Plato, The Republic

# Contents

# Foreword

*OUR SCHOOL* is an important book. It brings to life, in the most vivid way, many of the issues about American education that in political debates are too often treated as abstractions. In place of the conventional rhetoric about what's right or wrong in the nation's schools, Sam Chaltain offers a close-up, beautifully observed account of a year in the life of just two of them. In many respects, these schools couldn't be more different. Both are in Washington, D.C., physically close to the epicenter of American power, though in most other respects a world away from it. One is a start-up charter in new premises, still working to define its identity and to catch its beat. The other is a long-established neighborhood school, filled with the memories of generations: a school where many former pupils now send their own children or grandchildren.

*Our School* looks into the hearts and through the eyes of the children, teachers, and families that make up these two communities. As his narrative unfolds, Sam Chaltain captures the feelings and motivations, personalities and relationships that define the lived experience of these schools. He shows us the anxieties and exhilarations, the frustrations and achievements that ebb and flow through every classroom, every day of every week throughout the year. In doing so, he gives us a vibrant, often poetic portrait of real life at school. In its essentials, of course, this is what life is like in all schools everywhere. And that's the point. Schools are living, breathing communities and if we want policies that improve them, we need to understand how they feel and how they work.

*Our School* is deftly interlaced with meditations on these larger policy questions: charters and traditional public schools, parental choice, testing and standards, tracking and differentiation. These are all proper things for policymakers to talk about and we do need policies that work. Too often, though, the high-altitude talk of league tables, test scores, markets, and competition loses sight of the grainy, vernacular character of teaching and learning on the ground. Effective systems of finance, organization, and accountability do matter. But they are not what education is, or what it is for.

Education is always and inevitably a personal and social process. For communities and their children, going to school isn't about raising national test scores or the merits of core standards. It's about social aspirations and personal opportunity, public hopes and private fears. In America, education is also meant to be about social entitlement and human rights. As Sam Chaltain puts it, school should be about giving everyone "an equal shot at success." If so, the culture of schools themselves could not be more important and public policies should support them in promoting these values.

What does that mean in practice? It means treating all students as unique individuals, each with their own strengths and weaknesses, passions and aversions. It means recognizing that no school is better than its teachers and that teaching is an expert and demanding profession, which involves much more than knowing a particular discipline. It's about coaching and mentoring, collaborating and inspiring, and handcrafting the curriculum to the needs of different learners. It means giving school principals and administrators the respect and discretion they need to innovate in how their schools are organized and to adapt their culture to the challenges and opportunities of the communities they actually serve.

For the most part, the current emphasis on testing and standardization does not do any of this. On the contrary, national and state policies often picture education as some sort of industrial process that can be best understood through performance statistics and balance sheets of inputs and outputs.

What *Our School* shows with passion and precision is that education is about real people leading real lives in real places. If school doesn't engage them, it doesn't work, no matter what the accountants and policymakers may say. That's what this book is really about and why it's so important for anyone who genuinely cares about schools, communities, and their children.

—Sir Ken Robinson, October 2013

# Summer

UNLIKE THE OTHERS, who set off in teams to look for the twigs, branches, and leaves they would weave together to capture the essence of their school, Kristin Scotchmer searched the ground around her, alone.

She could count on one hand the moments she'd been completely alone since deciding to start a new school from scratch. But now it was June, and the inaugural year was over, and the staff of the Mundo Verde Bilingual Public Charter School was completing its last shared activity before the official start of the summer, when the size of their team would double, when they would transport all the records and wires and playthings and poster boards to a new building across town, and when the glow of what had just been accomplished would start to fade in exchange for a renewed anxiety of all the new challenges to be overcome.

Kristin leaned down and grabbed a branch, thin and moldable. This spot of Rock Creek Park was right next to the place she'd gone running all year to maintain her sense of balance—the only time of the week when no one could demand anything of her, and there was no problem to solve.

The teams returned to the clearing by the creek. Molly Howard was feeling ready for the year to be over. Berenice Pernalete was thinking about her summer adventure in Madrid that was just days away. And Dahlia Aguilar was steeling herself to be one of the ones to get in the water, because that's what her dad would have expected of his Dolly.

Before walking to the park from the school, which would soon revert to being just another floor in a downtown office building, Romey

Pittman had shown them the artwork of Andy Goldsworthy. Each image she shared framed evanescent sculptures Goldsworthy made with only the materials nature provided: circles of reconstituted icicles; potholes along a stream filled with bright yellow dandelions; lines of white wool along a dark stone fence.

The group decided their sculpture would be a circle of branches, to reflect the spirit of the Oglala Lakota poem Dahlia had given them:

> *In the Circle, we are all equal*
> *When in the Circle.*
> *No one is in front of you.*
> *No one is behind you.*
> *No one is above you.*
> *No one is below you.*

Some bent stacks of sticks into shape, while others wove together the many gradients of green—grass, leaves, brush—into a long, crooked line that would, they decided, form a path to lay across the center of the circle. It was always the same, Romey thought as she watched these young women work, remembering the first cabin she and her husband had built, and then lost to a fire the night they moved in: you gather your materials, you consult your plans, you make your decisions, and then you build the house.

The Bancroft Elementary School parade began in a small park at the confluence of five streets and three neighborhoods, and in the shadow of three different church spires. For months the weather had been cooler than usual, but by a mid-morning in June it was still hot enough to keep most of the adults huddled under the shade of the park's aging trees, each group swapping stories in a different mother tongue: Vietnamese, Spanish, Amharic, English. A police car idled at the base of the street that bore the name of the neighborhood it served—Mount Pleasant—and waited for the parade to begin.

As her teachers orchestrated the final arrangements—cheerleaders up front, drum and bugle corps to follow, and flag bearers representing every nation in the community picking up the rear—nine-year-old Lourdes adjusted the yellow "Nuestra Escuela" T-shirt across her slight shoulders and grabbed hold of the large, wide Bancroft banner with three other students. As they walked to the front of the line, past a sea of adults holding cameras and camcorders, Lourdes knew not to look for familiar faces. She wouldn't see her dad until later that summer, in Texas, and she had learned long ago it was best not to think about where Mami might be at any given moment. She watched the spinning lights at the top of the police car and imagined the parade was already over so she could be back on the soccer field, blazing down the sideline past all the boys to score another goal and show everyone how strong she really was.

The police car started crawling up the street, and the cheerleaders began their rhythmic chant: BAN-CROFT! The last remaining students and adults emerged from the shade of the trees to fall in line, while a phalanx of mothers with younger children formed an impromptu stroller brigade at the back.

Lourdes watched the people gathering in interest as the parade progressed down the street. Three heads poked out of a window above the 24-hour laundromat. A man with a lathered face got out of his chair to stand on the top step of the Pan American barbershop. An elderly woman sipped coffee from the porch of her aging Victorian, while younger children weaved their tricycles in between the foot traffic of the sidewalk.

As they reached the midway point of the street, Lourdes could see the white canopies of the neighborhood farmer's market—just past the Best World supermarket on one side of the street, and the blackened facade of the burned-out apartment building on the other.

Two blocks away, Zakiya Reid was preparing the back of the school for the parade's arrival. Parent volunteers set up the barbeque pit and sorted the hamburgers, hot dogs, and churros for quick cooking. Another group set up the moon bounce just beyond the dunking booth—her students always loved the chance to drop their principal into a tank of cold water.

Ms. Reid listened for the sound of the drums.

The year had not gone the way she had hoped. She'd endured a painful public challenge to her leadership. She'd struggled to gain support from her staff for a new style of classroom teaching. And she'd learned that two of her best in that new style, "the Two Rebeccas," would not be returning. Yet there were days like this that always seemed to come along at just the right time to remind her why she became an educator—days when a neighborhood's children and families would come together and remind each other that they were participating in the same dream: to unite all the children of a single community under a single roof in order to give them all an equal shot at success.

Imagine a year in the life of two different communities—a public charter school that was opening its doors for the very first time, and a neighborhood public school that first opened its doors in 1924.

In the fall of 2011, I embarked on a yearlong observation of these two schools, and of the city they exist to serve: Washington, D.C.

Like other major American cities, the nation's capital is experimenting with a new concept that is dramatically reshaping public education—school choice. In the past, choosing a school for their children was something only the wealthy could do; the rest of us merely enrolled in our neighborhood school and hoped for the best. Now, however, in cities like D.C., lower- and middle-class parents are considering a wider set of options—and confronting a wider array of obstacles. Although less than 3% of America's schoolchildren attend charter schools—public institutions with greater freedom to pilot different approaches to teaching, learning, and governance—44% of D.C.'s students are enrolled in such schools, including brand-new ones like Mundo Verde. At the same time, many of the city's traditional public schools are receiving an increasing number of applications from families that live outside its neighborhood boundaries. In the 2011–2012 school year, for example, nearly half of Bancroft's students lived outside its attendance zone.

Consequently, although the majority of children in rural and suburban America still attend their neighborhood schools, fewer and fewer urban families are doing so, opting instead to enter the chaotic and nascent marketplace of school choice, and participating in a great intra-city migration of families, each in search of a community to claim as their own.

This move toward greater school choice is particularly vital—and potentially dangerous—when one considers that public education is the only institution in American society that is guaranteed to reach 90% of every new generation, that is governed by public authority, and that was founded with the explicit mission of preparing young people to be thoughtful and active participants in a democratic society.

In this new frontier, will the wider array of school options help parents and educators identify better strategies for helping all children learn—strategies that can then be shared for the benefit of all schools? Or will the high stakes of the marketplace lead us to guard our best practices, undermine our colleagues, and privatize this most public of institutions?

I have written *Our School* because I believe that before we can answer these questions, we must put a human face on the modern landscape of teaching and learning. We must experience modern American schooling as today's teachers, students, and families do. And we must pay close attention to our changing notions of community, democracy, and choice.

How can greater choice bring us closer to one another, and to a revitalized notion of civic virtue and egalitarianism? How can we ensure that school choice does not contribute to an even wider divide between the haves and the have-nots, and an even wider discrepancy between those who know how to negotiate the increasingly commodified assets of modern life, and those who are merely left to take whatever comes their way? And how can our ongoing efforts to improve our schools reflect this basic truth about democracy—that while it does not require perfect equality, it does require that citizens share in a common life, one that is grounded as much in the "we" as the "me"?

The specific landscape of school choice may be new, but the general challenge is as old as the country itself: *E Pluribus Unum*—out of many, one.

# PART I

# FALL

## CHAPTER ONE

# The First Day

◇   ◇   ◇   MV   ◇   ◇   ◇

THE MORNING OF HER FIRST day as a first-year teacher in a first-year school, Molly Howard locked the door of her studio apartment in Dupont Circle, chatted briefly with the friendly doorman in her building, and walked several blocks west to her new job—directly against the grain of her former colleagues, and her former life.

They were there across the street to remind her, perpendicular to her path, walking north to south: women in fancy suits and flip flops on their way to K Street consulting jobs. Molly felt jubilant as she crossed New Hampshire Avenue and watched them disappear from view. It was one of those jobs that first brought her to D.C., right after graduating from Yale. Her goal was to save the world, and environmental policy seemed like a good place to start. Yet after two years on the job, all she'd learned was how to make attractive binders, and how long it would take her to rise up the ladder. She'd never been so unhappy. So she decided it was time for a change.

Molly neared the street-level entrance to Mundo Verde, which was spending its first year on the second floor of an office building that was still weeks away from finalizing a long-overdue punch list of renovations. Her phone rang. "I'm worried about you," her mother said. "I'll be fine," she answered. She'd slept soundly the night before. She was ready.

Molly walked up the steep concrete stairwell to the school, past a patchwork of electrical tape, hanging wires, and homemade signs welcoming children and families to their new school. No families had arrived yet—the school day didn't officially begin for another 90 minutes—but as she entered the room, *her* room, it occurred to her that the mere existence of a space in which to welcome people was its own cause for celebration.

Two days earlier, the hallways were abuzz with last-minute preparations. Workmen installed new windows in every room—a task the school's executive director, Kristin Scotchmer, had begged the building's owner to complete for weeks. Volunteers made their way up and down the hallways, using green markers and stencils to affix room numbers. The white-haired father of the school's board chair installed wire rods on the wall above the school's welcome desk, from which three colorful Mundo Verde T-shirts would hang. And boxes of furniture waited to be unpacked and arranged in the main central space they would call the *Zocalo*.

All signs of the recent chaos were long gone by the time Molly sat down at the tiny chair behind her tiny half-moon desk. She slid the laptop out of her backpack and opened it to review her plans for the day a final time. There was nothing left to do but wait.

When her alarm clock went off the morning of the first day—6:50 A.M. as always, and always the annoying beeping sound because nothing else would rouse her from her deep sleep—Rebecca Lebowitz hopped out of bed and into the 17-minute routine she had honed over her previous two years of being a teacher: Bathroom. Teeth. Face. Makeup. Seven minutes. Then six minutes to get dressed and four minutes to find her keys, grab her lunch, and head out the door to cross Meridian Hill Park—or, as it's been known locally since becoming a frequent site for political demonstrations in the 1960s, Malcolm X Park.

Four years earlier, Rebecca was a senior student at Brown, and Michelle Rhee was the freshman chancellor of D.C.'s public schools. When Lebowitz saw the December *Time* magazine cover of Rhee holding a broom and promising to clean house, she decided the nation's capital was where she'd start her career. Under Rhee's leadership, Lebowitz believed D.C. had a chance to show the rest of the country what was possible when an urban school system decided to judge teachers by their merits, to set high expectations for everyone, to up the level of rigor in urban classrooms, and to help the kids that had been most poorly served in the past by refusing to keep doing things the way they'd been done before.

She got placed at an elementary school in Mount Pleasant named after the founder of the U.S. Naval Academy: George Bancroft. It was a bumpy beginning. Six weeks into her first year, she was switched from first to third grade to replace a teacher who'd had a nervous breakdown in front of the children. Since then, she'd had two relatively stable years to hone her craft, and she felt like she was starting to warrant the praise she often received. Yet as she turned onto the long, sunny sidewalk that stretched in front of the three front doors of the only place she'd ever worked, Ms. Lebowitz felt increasingly certain that this year would be her last.

She entered the school's weathered gymnasium to search for her co-teacher, Rebecca Schmidt—together they were known as "the Two Rebeccas"—and meet the 60 third-graders they would soon escort up the spiral stairs, past the main office and the colorful mural depicting Columbus's arrival in the new world, to room 121. Children as young as three and as old as 11 stood or sat in clumps across the gym floor, waiting to be escorted to their homerooms. Parents received last-minute registration and information forms, while interpreters moved back and forth between groups to make sure each family understood what was required.

Near the gym's front door, Ms. Lebowitz approached a young boy she'd heard the second-grade teachers complain about last year. "How you doing, Harvey?" she said, smiling and putting an arm around his shoulder. "Did you have a great summer?" Harvey shrugged and remained silent, his head down. Nearby, two girls smiled at each other— new friends perhaps?—each still holding with one hand the leg of her father, each performing her own distinct pirouette.

As Rebecca Schmidt waited for her friend and co-teacher to arrive, she scanned the faces filling the gymnasium. A pack of boys twitched with Puckish energy and abandon near a girl receiving final words of encouragement from her grandmother, still dressed in the traditional dress and headscarf of their home country. A young woman entered the gym with her four sons in tow while a group of children were already busy trading pencils and swapping stories of summer fun. It was like an airport terminal—people of all shapes and colors, some reuniting, others struggling to say goodbye.

Rebecca Schmidt loved airport terminals. Ever since she'd been a kid, following her father's military postings around the world, she craved the sorts of spaces where you were either going somewhere exciting or being met by someone you love. As she waited for her new crop of third-graders to gather, Ms. Schmidt felt more hopeful than she had her previous four years as a teacher. After two years of working together, she and Ms. Lebowitz finally knew what they were doing when it came to teaching kids, *really* teaching them, to read and write. And that summer, they'd been informed that everyone coming into their class was reading on grade level—an unprecedented accomplishment, especially in a city where the overall proficiency rate was less than 50%.

In response, the Two Rebeccas had spent the summer planning for a very different sort of school year. They bought a slew of new books— beautiful, challenging books: fiction and non-fiction—and spent the final weeks of August arranging their room and establishing a library that would be both inviting and well matched to the levels and interests of their kids. Ms. Schmidt sat on the bottom step of the bleachers and ran her fingers around the spout of the electric kettle she'd brought in to make tea each morning, imagining the many success stories that lay ahead.

◊   ◊   ◊   **MV**   ◊   ◊   ◊

Berenice Pernalete put the phone back in her pocket and sat near the window of the Metro car as it passed above the Potomac River on its way out of Virginia and into D.C. Every morning, Berenice called her mother in Venezuela for some *Jarabe de lengua*—word medicine. Some days they talked about family members, or the latest news from home, or God. That morning, they talked about the opportunities associated with joining a brand-new school, and Berenice's plans to make it the best in the city at teaching young children to speak Spanish.

The train entered the Dupont Circle station, and Berenice stepped onto the escalator and scanned the crowd for children wearing Mundo

Verde T-shirts. A smile goes a long way, she thought, recalling what it felt like to attend a new school and not understand a single word that was said.

Ironically, it was the happiest time of her life. Her family had moved from Caracas to Houston. Berenice was 10 and knew nothing of America; she thought it was the name of her school. Everything smelled new on that first day, including the lunchbox in which her mom had placed handwritten cards of all the English expressions she'd need to safely make it home again.

Because of her light complexion, Berenice's homeroom teacher didn't realize the new girl didn't speak English until midday. But the new girl was already hard at work. We're only here for two years, her parents had told her in the days before the start of the school year. Use that time to speak English. Don't hang out with the other Spanish-speakers. Figure out who the smartest kids are—and mimic what they do.

She was fluent by Thanksgiving break.

Since then, Berenice had grown increasingly fascinated by the ways people learn a new language. It had been a long and winding road to the classroom—in Venezuela, it was cooler to dream of being a journalist or a TV producer, and she had already given both a try— but as she crossed the busy maze of cars and buses that filled Connecticut Avenue to reach the front doors of Mundo Verde, Berenice felt she was on the verge of the best year of her professional life—as long as the chaos of her school's inaugural year didn't drown out everything else.

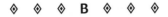

Zakiya Reid updated the enrollment numbers on her clipboard as homeroom after homeroom filed out of the gym and into the wide hallways of her school. Things always changed over the summer— families moved, families changed their minds, families got deported— and the first day of school was Ms. Reid's first chance to get a more accurate head count. It was the least interesting part of her job as a public school principal—with the most important ramifications. School budgets were determined by student enrollment, so until Ms. Reid knew how many bodies she had in the building, she couldn't know how much money she'd have to spend on them.

Over the summer, Ms. Reid had spent her time obsessing over a different number: 38. That was the percentage of children at Bancroft reading at or above grade level. She wondered what her grandma would say if she were still alive, but she knew it would be direct and honest; something like: "I don't mean you no harm, but . . . what in the hell are y'all doing at that school?"

Ms. Reid wished she still had her grandma's advice to manage the year ahead. Mabel Ezekiel had raised two daughters out of nothing and both had earned PhDs. She always knew how to push people, and she never got caught up in how people felt about her. Do what you have to do, and don't apologize for it.

A year ago Ms. Reid had tried to do just that after learning about the Reading & Writing Project in New York City, and seeing what it had done for children and schools across the country. This wasn't some fad of the moment; it was a proven model that had been applied by well-trained teachers in schools across the country for decades. I can't guarantee that our families will read to their children at night, she thought. But I *can* guarantee that our school is staffed by teachers who know how to help kids fall in love with language.

It was the kind of choice her grandma would have encouraged her to make. And she'd made it, knowing it was going to ruffle some feathers, especially after replacing a woman who'd been Bancroft's principal for the previous two decades. Change was always difficult in schools; asking teachers to change what they'd been doing over the course of their entire careers was something else entirely. Yet when she heard folks speak nostalgically about the way Bancroft used to be, she'd think, *That's great . . . but we have a 38% reading proficiency!*

Ms. Reid watched as the last homeroom left the gymnasium and updated the enrollment chart on her clipboard. She touched her belly instinctively, the baby inside her still too small to be felt.

◇  ◇  ◇  **MV**  ◇  ◇  ◇

In the new apartment she'd moved into after the separation that was a long time coming, Dahlia Aguilar closed the bathroom door and quietly got herself ready so her young son could grab a few more minutes of sleep. She looked across the street at the buildings of the Walter Reed Medical Hospital, selected the outfit for her first day as a principal—blue shirt, tan pants, and sneakers—and thought back to the apartment in Corpus Christi she'd lived in as a child, the one on 6th Street with the roaches and the gunfire.

That's where the wanting had begun; it started the first time she visited a friend's house on Ocean Drive. "Why don't we have that?" she remembered thinking. "How can I get that?"

Her dad saw the change in his oldest daughter's face in the following weeks—saw the building anger and resentment. There's a difference between being schooled and being smart, he said. Education is a bridge or a border. Choose.

As a child, Dahlia often fished with her father. Leave it there, her dad would tell her when she recast too quickly. Wait it out, Dolly, wait until it tugs. Learn to distinguish between the tide and a fish pulling on the lure.

One time she felt a tug that left no doubt. Her father watched the rod dip. She tried to pull back with enough force.

Daddy, I can't do this.

Don't ever say that.

The rod dipped lower and lower. Dahlia's father got behind her, added his hands to the pole and screamed, REEL IT IN!

The child strained as hard as she could until a stingray emerged, its wings wider than the rowboat in which they sat. The father grabbed it before it could strike and pinned it on the floor of the tipping craft. He reached in his boot for a pair of pliers, pulled the stinger off, and bellowed at his daughter to pull the hook out.

In seconds the ray was back out of the boat and struggling back down into the Gulf's greenish waters. Father and daughter lay there, exhausted and breathing hard. She felt like crying and laughing, then and now. He was always getting her into situations like that—situations that were bigger than she could handle—and then pushing her through them. *That's what kept him alive*, she thought as she rustled her son from colorful four-year-old dreams. *He was making sure I had some of it in me.*

◊   ◊   ◊   **MV**   ◊   ◊   ◊

By 8:15 A.M., half of Molly Howard's students were still missing. The new arrivals uneasily weaved toward the pegs near the door to hang up their backpacks. Molly entertained the others by persuading them to join her in a can-can line. She moved with energy and joy, her long arms active and welcoming. The students' faces tilted up to closely watch the strange new woman with the narrow glasses and the wide eyes.

Students were still filing in at 8:30 A.M., but Molly began the day promptly. "Alright friends, let's have everyone join me at the carpet calmly, quietly, and with everyone under control."

Most of the children followed right away; one boy still clung to his mother. She leaned down to give him a final squeeze, and then another. Molly's co-teacher, a calm young teacher-in-training named Jen, inched closer to sit nearby. The boy shifted his grasp to a full-waist hug, one eye on Jen. She modeled a deep breath for him by lifting her shoulders and letting out a long exhale.

The boy's grip loosened, and the mom left; he cried weakly. As Molly explained to the rest of the class how their morning meeting time would work, Jen knelt in front of him, speaking quietly so only he could hear.

◊   ◊   ◊   **B**   ◊   ◊   ◊

"In our class," Ms. Schmidt explained, "we'll start every day here, on the carpet, in a circle. This will be a space where we greet each other, get to know each other, and build a bridge from wherever we've been earlier in the morning to wherever we want to go together later in the day."

Ms. Schmidt sat on a chair at the base of a carpet, encircled by 30 nine-year-olds who formed a human frame for the rug's colorful map of the United States. "Today we'll start simply, by greeting each other and learning each other's names."

Ms. Schmidt watched as her new students rose hesitantly to introduce themselves and shake the hand of someone else in the circle.

Over the years she'd come to believe that the time they took each morning for these sorts of non-academic endeavors was more valuable than anything else she did as a teacher. It was, in her mind, the way school was supposed to be—a safe space in which children could learn about themselves and each other, and a ritualized place in which the anger and anxieties of the more troubled students could be surfaced and released.

Sitting across from her at a cluster of student desks, Rebecca Lebowitz was not so sure. She'd always rolled her eyes at the touchy-feely stuff. She'd also been trained to focus exclusively on academic growth and backward planning. The mark of a good teacher was having strict expectations and clear consequences—and translating those into measurable progress in a student's ability to learn. Not once in her training had she learned about the merits of building a sense of community in the classroom. She admired efficiency in herself and in others, and a morning meeting about a group of children's non-academic thoughts and feelings was anything but efficient.

She'd heard the arguments—that the social curriculum is as important as the academic curriculum, and that how children learn is as important as what they learn. She'd also seen ways in which the ritualized morning time had paid off for some of their most troubled students over the past two years. Those were the students that drove her—the boys and girls who'd been ignored or forgotten or overlooked for too many years of their young lives. And it was thinking of their possible futures that made her wonder about the redemptive limits of learning to cooperate; what those children needed most to escape the cycle of poverty was to learn how to read.

Ms. Schmidt asked for a volunteer to read the morning message to the class, while Ms. Lebowitz scanned the faces in the room, searching for early clues about the children that were now in their care.

◇  ◇  ◇  MV  ◇  ◇  ◇

By midday, when Kristin Scotchmer peered through the window of Berenice's classroom to check in on the Zebras, she noticed no one was eating.

"*¡A comer!*" Berenice repeated as a boy stuffed books under his shirt, while another leaned dangerously back in his chair next to a quiet girl sucking her thumb. The lunches sat largely untouched.

Kristin knew Berenice could take care of herself; she was one of the school's most experienced hires. Yet it was also clear that two very different tones were already emanating from the two kindergarten classrooms.

Over the summer, Kristin had randomly divided Mundo Verde's five-year-olds into two sections: the Lions and the Zebras. As a bilingual school, the plan was for the sections to alternate days between the Spanish and English classrooms. Thus far, the Lions were quietly cruising along without much interruption in English; but the Zebras were presenting a cacophony of challenges for Ms. Berenice to confront. Kristin wondered if the relative lack of Spanish spoken in the homes of her families might explain the stark contrasts between the two rooms, or if it was something different about Molly's or Berenice's approach. Time would tell.

"*Para, mira y escucha,*" Berenice sang, trying to transition the group into some form of cleanup. Bodies spun around her in a miniature ballet.

◊   ◊   ◊   **MV**   ◊   ◊   ◊

At 3:30 P.M., Berenice opened the door of her classroom to signal the end of the day. She smiled weakly as the *Zocalo* grew loud with the voices of adults and children.

Kristin stood at the top of the stairwell, greeting families in Spanish and English. She felt this was her most important job as executive director: providing a face for the parents, answering any and all questions, and freeing up Dahlia to focus on the needs of the faculty. The queue of families stretched all the way down the stairwell and out the front door. Kristin marveled once again at the trust that had been placed in her.

It had been five years since the idea for Mundo Verde first surfaced in the minds of Kristin and a few other parents. They all had children at the same Quaker preschool, and as they started looking for schools, they realized that a lot of what they all sought wasn't out there. Kristin was not an educator, and she didn't know much about charters at the time, though what she knew was generally critical. She'd heard the claims that charters skimmed the best students off the top of the public school system, siphoned valuable dollars away from the neighborhood schools that needed them most, and provided a way for corporate entities to establish moneymaking ventures where they didn't belong. Yet as she expanded her own research and investigated the uneven landscape of D.C. schools, the thing she kept noticing was that the charter schools always seemed to be the places with the most vitality and diversity. Some were clearly better than others, but all of them seemed to benefit from the fact that everyone there, from the staff to the families, had opted *into* something.

Then Kristin saw the length of their waiting lists, and she realized the city could open as many as 50 new schools and still not meet the demand they were generating. For the first time, she started to imagine leaving her work at a non-profit and actually trying to start a school from scratch.

Kristin and her partners—a core group of 12—spent the next several months meeting over potluck dinners and glasses of wine. They researched real schools and dreamed of ideal ones. And then, after a year and a half of hard work, they deployed a team member to deliver the meticulously crafted 100-page application to the city's authorizing body, the Public Charter School Board (PCSB)—only to learn an hour later that their team member had gotten stuck in traffic, and the application had arrived too late to be considered. No excuses.

The news was devastating—and it got worse when they learned the PCSB would not accept any new applications the following year. That meant that by the time the elementary school they'd spent the past two years dreaming up could actually receive a charter and open its doors, another two years would have to pass. And that meant that Kristin's children—and the children of the other founding families— would all be too old to attend it.

Over another potluck dinner, the team asked a new question: Do we believe in this model because it would be great for *our* kids, or are we trying to make the best possible school for *all* kids?

Kristin held bits and pieces of that journey in her mind as she chatted with a grandmother lingering at the school's front door, near the bowl of apples children reached into as they left. "We want this to be a place where kids can learn through play and the things that are relevant to their lives," she explained. "And that's why I think the charter model is so powerful. When you start with questions like 'why not' or 'what if,' everything becomes possible."

◊   ◊   ◊   **MV**   ◊   ◊   ◊

By five o'clock, the hallways of Mundo Verde were empty again except for the teachers and staff. Kristin retreated to the office she shared with three other people to review some of the logistical issues that had proven harder than they'd expected, like organizing snack time or getting the children to and from the nearby park for recess.

Dahlia Aguilar walked through the hallways to invite everyone to join her in the *Zocalo* for an end-of-day celebration. She smiled as she spoke, reflecting an energy the teachers were unable to match. "The only way to end our first day is with a party!" said Dahlia. "Everyone, please come and join me."

The staff rose and arranged themselves in a circle. Most of them wore Mundo Verde T-shirts; almost all of them were young women in their first or second year of teaching. Dahlia had worked in schools for more than a decade, and she knew how exhausting the first day could feel. Teaching had its own form of conditioning, and no form of summer study could prepare you for the grind of standing on your feet for seven hours without a single break.

"This is a party for people who ate lunch today," she began. "Who gave someone a pause or a timeout today. Who taught someone something valuable. For anyone who hugged someone else. And this is a party to celebrate the ways we lived up to our mission."

Dahlia looked around at the faces in the circle. She'd planned a few other closing exercises, but she could see that the best decision was simply to let people go home. "Thank you all for what you did to successfully launch this school. You were wonderful today. I'll see you tomorrow morning."

◇   ◇   ◇   **B**   ◇   ◇   ◇

As the last of their aftercare students ran out of the room to head for home in the final strips of sunlight, Ms. Lebowitz turned to her co-teacher pointedly. "Is it just me, or is this not a classroom of kiddos reading on grade level?"

Ms. Schmidt looked up from the desk and reluctantly grunted her agreement. Before her was a colorful stack of "Hopes and Dreams for Third Grade"—an exercise they always did at the beginning of the year to learn about each child's interests and outlook. A few of the notes seemed age-appropriate, like Francesca's wish "to go to the Baltimore museum and see the dolfin show," or Jonny's modest hopes to "play outside." Then there was Noemi's aspirational goal, expressed in nearly unintelligible spelling: "I hope to lun to slpel wrs because a m ging to go te colejig." And then there was Rodger, a fragile, thickly bespectacled boy, whose dream was merely unintelligible: "Matlattrusala is big. You like Matlatirusla."

"It does seem like something may have gotten lost in the translation of what we were told," Ms. Schmidt added as she changed into her running shoes. "But let's give it some time. We don't need to reinvent everything yet."

## CHAPTER TWO

# Out of Many

◊   ◊   ◊   **B**   ◊   ◊   ◊

IT'S NOT EVEN NOON on a late September morning, and Harvey is already back on the floor.

Ms. Schmidt continues framing the mini-lesson for the rest of the class, while Harvey's tablemates wait for Ms. Lebowitz to arrive and restore order. His pear-shaped body slumps on the carpet as he chews his necklace and waits for her to arrive.

"Let's get back into it," she says, rubbing his back to coax him up to the table. Harvey picks up his book, and Ms. Lebowitz resumes scanning the faces of the other 29 students. Mid-morning light cuts across the classroom from the large windows that line the east wall, casting lines of shadow on the homemade emoticon plates to which each child attaches a clothespin to register his or her daily mood: sad, angry, worried, frustrated, frightened, excited, bored, happy.

"As we go into independent reading," Ms. Schmidt instructs, "remember to look in your books for the different elements of a story." A piece of butcher paper behind her provides further guidance:

Elements of a Story

*Somebody*—who/what is the main character?
*Wanted*—what does s/he want?
*But*—what gets in the way?
*So*—how does the main character respond?

At one set of desks, Elliott disappears into his book before Ms. Schmidt finishes her instructions. Pale and quiet, his hair still bearing

*17*

the shape of last night's sleep, Elliott is an avid reader; over the summer he finished more than 20 books, from *The Hobbit* to *The Trumpet of the Swan*. Ms. Lebowitz walks between the desks and sees him reading intently. She transfers her attention to a different table where her presence is more sorely needed.

While Ms. Lebowitz works the room, Ms. Schmidt sits at their desk reviewing the class's initial diagnostic literacy tests. It's her first chance to see if the reports she received over the summer about the incoming third-graders were true. And it's worse than she thought: just 5% are reading on grade level.

Three out of 60.

Ms. Schmidt's body shook with both anger and sadness. Then she wondered why she felt surprised. In her five years as a teacher, if there was anything she'd learned it was that there are the things students *should* be learning in third grade, and then there are the things that represent where they really are in their development.

Schmidt's eyes lifted up to survey the classroom; she watched as Ms. Lebowitz helped a young girl named Lourdes sound out words on a page. Then she returned her attention to the report in front of her and looked closer at the results.

Like a lot of schools, Bancroft classifies its students' reading levels by an A–Z letter system named for the system's co-founders, Irene Fountas and Gay Pinnell. In use for years by schools across the country, the A–Z rating was initially no more than a way for teachers to identify appropriately leveled books for each child; over time, it evolved to also name specific behaviors and understandings for each level that teachers could be on the lookout to notice, teach for, and support. It was, in effect, a road map for teachers like the Two Rebeccas to follow in steering their students to literacy.

Helping kids learn how to read was what led Rebecca Schmidt to become a teacher in the first place. After graduating from Grinnell with a double major in psychology and women's studies, she had, like most 21-year-olds, no idea what to do next. But she knew she had to start *somewhere*, and because her parents had recently settled down in D.C. after a life spent abroad, she followed them.

Soon thereafter, rather haphazardly, she got her first job working for a reading research company. Up to that point, Ms. Schmidt had never seriously considered teaching. But that summer she spent day after day providing intensive one-on-one tutoring, for hours at a time, with children who could not read, and who 12 weeks later had learned how. It was exhausting and life changing, for them and for her. And she realized that although the work she was doing was important, the real place it needed to be happening was not in some summer program, but in a full-time, yearlong classroom, day in and day out.

Schmidt checked Elliott's score: an N, which put him right in line with the projected N–P continuum for a third-grader. Good. Then she scanned the vertical column of letters to get a feel for the class as a whole. Two other students, both girls, also read at N level: the rest— students like Harvey and Lourdes—were a flood of Cs, Ds, and Gs— the sorts of levels you were supposed to see in kindergarten. And a few, like Rodger, had a two-letter score, "RB." For those students, the path to literacy didn't begin with independent reading or vocabulary study; it began with learning basic "Reading Behaviors," like how to hold a book right side up.

Ms. Schmidt wanted to scream. How the hell did these students make it to third grade without anyone raising alarm bells? And what the hell are we going to do about it now?

Later that day, after school, the Two Rebeccas stayed late to plot a course of action. They redid the library they'd spent the summer assembling. They redrew the list of books they'd chosen for read-alouds throughout the year. And they began strategizing about how they could meet the needs of students like Elliott, who was already halfway through the *Harry Potter* series, alongside students like Harvey, who couldn't sit in his seat long enough to even open a book, let alone read it.

Ms. Schmidt knew from past experience that every school year evolved like this one—with rapid real-time calculations and recalculations, spot assessments, and information that laid waste to the best-laid plans. Yet the disconnect between what she'd been told over the summer and what she discovered within the first weeks of the school year left her feeling more enervated than usual. It was hard enough to do her job really well; all the extra noise and dysfunction in the system was starting to make it feel Sisyphean.

The next morning, she was back at the front of the room, watching as Ms. Lebowitz tried to help Harvey stay focused through a math lesson. Ms. Schmidt glanced at the broken clock on the wall above them: 1:35. Then she pulled out her smartphone: 10:15.

◊   ◊   ◊   **MV**   ◊   ◊   ◊

Ms. Molly didn't see the scissors sail past the head of their target, but she heard the sound of them hitting the wall. She grabbed Bruno by the hand and escorted him to the carpet to cool down, her cheeks red at the thought of a different outcome. Molly looked around quickly at the other children in the room, wondering where the next outburst would come from, and when she would feel like she'd know what to do when it did.

The school year was only a few weeks old, but Molly already knew she needed extra energy on the days she had the Zebras. The luck of the draw had placed many of the children with the greatest needs— from intellectual to social to emotional—in the same section. That meant that on the days the Zebras had English, Molly could expect to walk a highwire of behavioral intervention from start to finish. And it meant that on the other days, Molly could expect to teach the Lions how to read and write.

"Why did you throw the scissors, Bruno? I want to understand what you were thinking so I can help you be safe." Molly sat cross-legged in front of the remorseless young boy, his body taut with resistance. She scanned the room to see how her other students were doing. A young girl with tousled hair named Freya sat quietly; amidst the stronger needs and personalities of the Zebras, Freya was already becoming a student whose needs were continually subjugated, and Molly knew it. But there simply wasn't enough time and energy to tend as closely to obedient children like Freya when the disobedient ones like Bruno were always a moment away from injuring themselves or someone else.

A few feet away at the edge of the carpet, another boy named Albert leaned way back in his chair. Molly turned toward him to remind him to correct his body. That's when Bruno took his fist and jammed it violently into his teacher's ear.

The sting of the punch spread in tingles across her face. She stepped into the hallway, adjusted her black glasses to wipe away the tears, and took a deep breath. As she opened the door to return to her classroom, a roomful of faces turned to greet her. Molly checked her watch. 10:15.

Across the hall, Dahlia Aguilar was wondering what to do to change the tone her young school was already starting to assume. Dahlia knew being a principal in a first-year charter school was going to have its share of surprises. What she hadn't expected was that so many of her teachers would be sending so many three-, four-, and five-year-old children to the office, so early in the year. She'd been an educator long enough to know that the little kids getting kicked out of class were likely to become the big kids dropping out of school. Something had to change, and quickly, before those children started living down to the expectations of a faculty that was as inexperienced as it was hardworking.

Dahlia could see the sort of place she wanted Mundo Verde to become—a place where every classroom was filled with supportive adults with clear expectations, and where discipline issues got turned into real-time learning opportunities that helped children learn about responsible behavior and how to regulate their own emotions. She believed what John Dewey had written almost a century ago—that the purpose of education is not to merely grant children freedom of activity or choice or movement, but to empower them with the freedom to engage in *intelligent* activity, to make *intelligent* choices, and to exercise *intelligent* self-control in identifying, and then acting upon, their unique strengths and interests. The mistake so many schools made was to see something like "discipline" as separate from or ancillary to that overall purpose.

Dahlia knew Mundo Verde's approach to discipline could not be ancillary; it would be a foundational part of what the school did to prepare children for success in the world and in life. What she didn't know was how to help her young staff *act* on that belief, especially now that the school year had begun and everything around them was unfolding at warp speed.

It wasn't even October, and already Dahlia had accepted the surprise resignation of one of her most experienced lead teachers, so unprepared was she for the challenges of teaching outside the relative calm of a suburban school. Everyone had done the best they could to plug the sudden gap and keep moving. But when Dahlia watched the ways in which the daily challenges of student behavior were impacting the stamina of her teachers, she wondered what else could be done.

It was a feeling she knew firsthand. One of the earliest recruits for Teach for America, Dahlia began her career as a young twentysomething educator at a struggling school in D.C. Her trial by fire started quickly when her principal assigned her all the Latino kids and called it a "bilingual class." Her colleagues took her new furniture and replaced it with their old stuff, leaving behind nothing but stacks of that damp green paper that always smelled like wet ink. Even her building felt like the sort of place people went to be forgotten. Once, it had been designed as an open space in which children could learn in a Montessori-like setting, their interests directing their activities. By the time Dahlia worked there, it was merely a big room filled with adults screaming at kids all day long.

Just as Molly was doing now, Dahlia had been forced to learn on the fly. How do you teach kids to read? How do you discipline them in constructive ways? She'd tried different approaches, organized gang outreach work and hosted afterschool poetry workshops. She purchased all her own materials and hauled them up Irving Street in a rickety grocery cart with wheels that sounded like a train squealing to a stop. And, gradually, after a few years, her students started graduating.

Dahlia watched from her office as Molly's class poured into the *Zocalo* to head to the park for recess. She walked into the hallway to meet her. "You OK?" the principal asked. "I don't even know," the teacher replied tersely, her cheeks still streaked with tears. "I have zero sense of what's normal."

What *is* normal when it comes to a modern-day American classroom? What should it be? And can one, two, or even three teachers in a room of 20 to 30 children not just maintain a sense of order, but also diagnose the needs of each child—and then meet those needs, consistently and measurably?

In theory, such a goal has always directed America's efforts to improve its public schools; after all, the first major federal legislation affecting public education was part of President Lyndon B. Johnson's equity-oriented "War on Poverty." But the goal was never explicitly stated—and incentivized—until 2002, when the 107th U.S. Congress rechristened Johnson's legislation the No Child Left Behind (NCLB) Act, and President George W. Bush heralded the dawn of "a new time in public education in our country. As of this hour," he said, just before signing the bill at a public high school in Ohio, "America's schools will be on a new path of reform, and a new path of results."

Under Bush's new path, all schools receiving federal funding would be required to annually test every child in certain grades in both reading and math. The students' scores would be broken down and reported by subgroups—both as a way to highlight the progress of historically under-served groups of children, and to ensure that no single group's performance could be concealed amidst a single, all-encompassing number. "The story of children being just shuffled through the system is one of the saddest stories of America," said Bush. "The first step to making sure that a child is not shuffled through is to test that child as to whether or not he or she can read and write, or add and subtract. . . . We need to know whether or not children have got the basic education. . . . And now it's up to you, the local citizens of our great land, the compassionate, decent citizens of America, to stand up and demand high standards, and to demand that no child—not one single child in America—is left behind."

By the start of the 2011–2012 school year, more than a decade after the passage of NCLB, Congress was still trying—and failing—to rewrite the law, and opinions remained split about whether it had been more helpful or hurtful to American schools. On one side, critics decry the bill's narrow focus on reading and math scores, and the ways it has had the unintended effects of squeezing other subjects out of the curriculum and stifling the creative capacity of teachers to engage their kids in different ways. On the other side, advocates celebrate the ways NCLB has forced America to publicly confront just how poorly some students have been served in the past. No Child Left Behind shone a data-drenched light on the actual academic differences between kids, they argue, and sunshine is the most powerful disinfectant with the potential to highlight the most necessary reforms.

Across the same general time frame, an equally seismic policy shift had occurred: the virtual disappearance of "tracking"—or the process of assigning students to classes based on categorizations of their perceived academic potential. In its place, today's teachers are increasingly expected to "differentiate" their lessons—and not merely to each class, but to each child, every day, all year long.

This constellation of forces—the dawn of high-stakes testing, the death of tracking, and the desirability of differentiated instruction—had engendered a perfect storm of reform that dramatically recast the daily experiences and expectations of teachers like Molly and the Two Rebeccas. And once again, education experts remained split over whether the forces at play were ultimately for the better.

"We are shortchanging America's brightest students," argues education scholar Frederick Hess, "and we're doing it reflexively and furtively. A big part of the problem is our desire to duck hard choices when it comes to kids and schooling. Differentiated instruction—the notion that any teacher can simultaneously instruct children of wildly different levels of ability in a single classroom—is appealing precisely because it seemingly allows us to avoid having to decide where to focus finite time, energy, and resources. The truth is, few teachers have the extraordinary skill and stamina to constantly fine-tune instruction to the needs of 20- or 30-odd students, six hours a day, 180 days a year. What happens instead is that teachers tend to focus on the middle of the pack. Or, more typically of late, on the least-proficient students.

"Focusing on the neediest students, even at the expense of their peers, is not unreasonable," Hess explains. "After all, we can't do everything. But self-interest and a proper respect for all children demand that we wrestle with such decisions and pay more than lip service to the needs of advanced students."[1]

Carol Ann Tomlinson, a nationally known expert on issues of differentiation, defines the issue differently: "Is the primary goal a separate room for students with particular needs, or should our primary goal be high-quality learning experiences wherever a student is taught? The range of students in schools indicates the need for a range of services. Since most students have always received most of their instruction in general education classrooms, it's quite important that differentiation in that setting be robust. There are some very bright students whose academic needs are quite well addressed in some 'regular' classrooms, some who require extended instruction in a specific subject, some whose need for challenge suggests specialized instruction in all content areas—perhaps even outside the student's school. Effective differentiation would serve the student in each of those situations."[2]

◇ ◇ ◇ **B** ◇ ◇ ◇

Of course, there are conversations about schooling that take place at 30,000 feet. And then there's the real work that takes place on the ground, in real time. That was where Ms. Lebowitz took advantage of an early afternoon break one day in September to draft a list of students she thought might be good candidates for special education services.

In theory, all such diagnoses would have occurred long before a student reached third grade. In practice, however, Ms. Lebowitz was always finding students who had been allowed to travel invisibly through the system and into her classroom. And inevitably, those students were always the ones who captured her heart.

Harvey was fast becoming one of those students. She'd seen boys like him before. Usually, they were Brown or Black. Mostly, they'd been passed from grade to grade like a baton no one wanted to hold for too long, slowly growing certain of their own undesirability. Somewhere along the path of her formal education, Ms. Lebowitz read there was even a name for that sort of institutionalized neglect: the "deadly fog"[3]—formed whenever the cold mist of adult cultural bias and ignorance obscured the warm vitality of children of color.

Harvey was definitely warm and vital. He also had trouble paying attention to anything that didn't involve playing with cars or drawing action figures with swords. Ms. Lebowitz started finding out what she could about him. She learned his parents had been divorced for some time, but that both were intent on playing an active role in his growth; they even attended parent/teacher conferences together. She learned the mother lived with a man whose temper often turned violent. And she learned that Harvey had been informally diagnosed with attention deficit disorder—but that aside from that there was no other paper trail to work from. More than once over the years, in fact, Harvey's paperwork had disappeared entirely. As a result, he'd never been formally tested, which meant he'd never been made eligible for the extra support services that are designed to help students with extra learning needs.

Now it was Ms. Lebowitz's turn to shake with anger. She bounded up the stairs to the third floor and the isolated office of the school's lone social worker, Valerie Flores.

"Did you know Harvey has never been tested?" she began.

"Don't get me started," Ms. Flores responded, sitting at her desk in front of a large farm-style sink that hinted at the room's previous use. "That boy scares people, when really all he needs is some love."

"I know! He's such a muffin. So what can we do about it?"

"Let's get him tested. You know what to do."

Although the extent of her training had only spanned a few weeks one summer, Ms. Lebowitz was one of the teachers at Bancroft best equipped to support students with special needs. She knew the first step in the process of getting a child tested was to identify a few immediate strategies she and Ms. Schmidt could try out to see if they led to any improvement, such as giving him more individual attention, or providing more tactile ways to experience a subject like math. If that didn't work, the teachers and Ms. Flores would meet again six weeks later to see if there were any other classroom interventions they could try. The last step would be a meeting with Harvey's parents to explain the situation and receive their consent to get him formally tested. Ms. Lebowitz collected his attendance and health records—what she could find, anyway—and made a folder with the few work samples that had already been generated since the start of the school year. The rest would have to wait.

Meanwhile, Ms. Flores called Harvey's mother. "Thank you so much for calling," his mom said when she answered. "I've been asking for years to get Harvey tested." Ms. Flores sighed. "I'm so sorry this hasn't happened sooner," she replied. "We're going to do everything we can to get your son the support he needs."

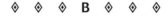 ◊ ◊ ◊ **B** ◊ ◊ ◊

When Valerie Flores first joined the staff of Bancroft three years earlier, she was part of a team of three professionals whose shared job was to support the social and emotional needs of the school's 500 children. By the 2011–2012 school year, thanks to budget cuts and tough decisions, she was the only one left.

Ms. Flores was not unfamiliar with dysfunction. As a Peace Corps teacher in Uzbekistan, she'd taught in a building that, like Bancroft's, was too cold in the winter, and too hot in the summer. She'd watched as her students were boarded on buses and taken out to the fields to pick cotton for the first part of the school year—without ever getting paid. And she'd remembered arriving at school one day to find her co-teacher furtively shoving a shipment of new books into a taxi. She called Peace Corps the same day to complain and inform them she wasn't coming back to work until the books came back. Three weeks passed before they did.

At Bancroft, Ms. Flores worked with kids and families from all over the world—El Salvador and Honduras, Ethiopia and the Far East. She worked with kids whose teeth were rotting and kids whose parents were millionaires. The challenge each day was to address everyone's needs, equally. And some days were better than others.

Thursdays were her favorite—no meetings, just kids coming to her office, sitting in the oversized playhouse or playing with her stack of toys or moving the limbs of her small mannequin, talking about their world. Ms. Flores would sit quietly and listen for sharp points in their stories on which to peg new ideas or possibilities or problem-solving skills. Sometimes it worked. Other times she'd marvel at how they'd made it as far as they had.

The other day, while standing outside the front of the school with Harvey, she watched as he greeted three cops who were walking by.

"How do you know those men?" she asked.

"They've all been to my house a bunch of times," he said casually. Ms. Flores pieced together the rest.

⬦   ⬦   ⬦   **MV**   ⬦   ⬦   ⬦

The day his mother was scheduled to come in and meet with Molly and Dahlia, Albert struggled more than usual.

The seeds were sown that morning during circle time. The Zebras were playing a warm-up game in which everyone sang the same refrain, "My mommy told me to tell you, to do my name just like I do," before different children would say their name and act out some movement to represent it. Then the group would say that child's name and mimic their movement, and the cycle would repeat. It was a way to help the children become more familiar with each other's names and mannerisms, and although Bruno and a few others skulked in a corner, most of the children swayed along happily, eyes bright with joy.

During the last round of the game, the order randomly landed on Albert. His countenance shifted as he smiled sheepishly, thrilled to have a turn in the spotlight. "Do I get to go?"

"You'll be first next time," Molly assured him, eager to move the group into the next activity. Albert's shoulders sunk. He clasped his hands behind his head and stared at the wall.

Molly tried to transition the class into silent reading, but Albert was lost for the day. He flicked through his book aggressively and put it down within seconds. "I'm done," he announced. "Read it again," Molly directed, her voice already strained.

Fifteen minutes later, while one boy rested his head on his book and another hid under a table, Molly was struggling to engage a headstrong little girl named Princess. When it became clear Princess was determined to refuse to do whatever was asked of her, Molly pulled out her phone and threatened to call Princess's mother. It worked; Princess plopped down on the carpet next to Albert, his face still scowling from that morning's perceived act of injustice.

Over those first weeks of the year, Molly had tried to take close notice of all her students. Some, like Bruno, seemed as if they'd already become hardened to the world around them. Others, like Freya, seemed less immediately affected by their surroundings, both at home and at school. They just floated along. And then there was Albert, who began each day with an acute sense of neediness and eagerness to please. Any slight—real or imagined—sent emotional waves crashing over the edges of his small lifeboat and left him flailing like a drowning boy.

Back at her apartment, Molly spent most evenings searching for explanations. Her small bookshelf was filled with titles promising to answer the most essential questions of her new profession: *The Skillful Teacher. The Classroom Teacher's Survival Guide. Teach Like a Champion. Read It Again. The Art of Teaching Reading. Can We Talk About Race?* Some authors skipped over the emotional obstacles to prescribe effective academic intervention strategies. Others left the academic issues un-touched in order to outline the developmental needs of children. And then there was the University of Arizona's Bruce Ellis, who suggested it all came down to a student's level of reactivity to the environment in which he or she lived. Some children are like dandelions, he said; oth-ers are like orchids. And whereas dandelions thrive under just about any condition, orchids require a much more delicate balance of condi-tions in order to grow.

As SUNY professor David Sloan has written, "This new informa-tion transforms, or should transform, educational practice. Orchid chil-dren don't need to be cured; they need to be placed in environments that enable them to bloom. And dandelion children won't necessarily respond to the enrichments that orchid children thirst for. These indi-vidual differences are not entirely genetically based. Perhaps it's pos-sible for orchid children to become dandelion children and vice versa, but it might not be as simple as exchanging a red shirt for a blue shirt. Moreover, children shouldn't necessarily be expected to change their strategies, any more than a tortoise should be expected to change into a hare. Our educational system needs to accommodate and capitalize on individual differences, not eliminate them."[4]

Some of those differences, it turns out, can be environmentally ex-plained. As Paul Tough reports in his bestselling book *How Children Succeed*, "It is in early childhood that our brains and bodies are most sensitive to the effects of stress and trauma. . . . The part of the brain most affected by early stress is the prefrontal cortex, which is critical in self-regulatory activities of all kinds, both emotional and cognitive. As a result," Tough explains, "children who grow up in stressful environ-ments generally find it harder to concentrate, harder to sit still, harder to rebound from disappointments, and harder to follow directions."[5]

Molly was hopeful the meeting with Albert's mother might il-luminate some of the conditions that would help him flourish. She watched as the woman—friendly, warm, and not much older than Molly—entered Dahlia's office just after 3:30 P.M. She sat down and bounced Albert's younger sister on her knee. "What do I need to know?" she asked.

"We're having trouble finding ways to support Albert at school," Dahlia began. Molly nodded, grateful she wasn't the one leading the conversation. How direct and forthcoming is one supposed to be in these sorts of meetings, and how do you make sure a parent doesn't feel defensive when you're talking about their child's struggles? That was the art of it—and she still felt very much like a beginner.

Albert's mother described an average night at their home. "He usually goes to bed around 11:00," she said. "I can't figure out how to get him down sooner," she volunteered, perhaps in search of her own source of mentoring.

"Children need a sense of predictability and ritual in their lives," Dahlia responded calmly. "Have you ever tried giving him a bath each night, and reading to him before he goes to sleep?"

"You think that will work?" the mom asked.

"I think it's worth a try," Dahlia offered, "though I want us to work together to see if there are other ways we can help him focus his energy. Is there anything you do at home that works particularly well? Perhaps we can try it here, too."

"Well, whenever I tell him he'll get to see his father if he behaves better, he shapes right up."

Dahlia felt tears well up in her eyes and quickly pulled them back. Earlier in the year, she'd learned that Albert had never met his father—and never would. She knew how deeply Albert yearned for a father; he spoke about him often, talked about how he would travel across the ocean to meet him one day, and asked his mom each morning when he was coming to visit. It was clear his mom had not thought through the ramifications of her empty promise. She had simply been desperate to corral him and relied on what she could.

"I think it's important not to give Albert false promises," Dahlia suggested. "We need to help him take charge of his own behavior, and we need to love him as much as we can. Maybe together we can work on establishing a clearer ritual, and on separating any feelings he has about his father with feelings about his own behavior?"

"I'll do whatever it takes," the mom responded. "Thank you so much for taking an interest in him."

Molly exited the meeting feeling surprised and discouraged. She thought about students like Albert—her orchid children—who were struggling with so many painful issues and emotions. She thought about dandelion children like Freya whose natures made them less problematic—and also less likely to stand out enough to receive any sustained individual attention. And she started to wonder, before the leaves from the trees had even started to fall, how she was going to sustain herself in such an emotionally weighted profession.

◊   ◊   ◊   **B**   ◊   ◊   ◊

Every night, after her workday was over, Zakiya Reid hung with her two children in the kitchen of their Hyattsville apartment. It was her favorite part of the day—they didn't care what challenges their mother had weathered, so those sensitive topics never came up. Instead, her five-year-old son would sit on the floor and play with the pots and pans, while she and her eight-year-old daughter would chat over a printed Internet recipe for that evening's dinner.

Lately, it was becoming harder for Ms. Reid to check the challenges of the day at the schoolhouse gate. It was her third year at Bancroft, and she was disappointed with the pace at which the school was changing. Although some of the most resistant teachers had moved on, she knew she hadn't yet effectively prepared and supported the people who remained. And while it was one thing to ask adults to start approaching their work differently, it was another entirely to do so before showing them how.

Ms. Reid rolled the drumsticks in a bowl to cover them with breading, the din of her son's cacophonous play barely registering in her mind. It had felt good to finally put her most direct thoughts and feelings out there with the faculty, despite the challenges it had brought. Her first year had been all about listening to what people felt and saw—and aligning that with what the numbers told her. Last year had allowed her to hint at the sort of changes she hoped to see in the school's approach to teaching and learning. This year, it was time for people to decide if they were down with the vision or not.

For Ms. Reid, the certainty of the path she was blazing felt reassuring. A math major in college, she'd always loved the certainty of numbers. That's what led her to take her first job at the IRS. But it didn't take long before she felt bored to death.

She'd never considered being a teacher; they didn't make enough money. But then she started volunteering as an afterschool teacher in

Georgetown. Before long she was using the workday to prepare for what she did when the workday was over, and realized that in her relationships with the children—unlike her relationships with her colleagues—she was getting as much as she was giving. If she didn't show up for work one day, nothing happened. But if she missed a day at afterschool, the kids noticed. She felt wanted and needed. So she decided to apply for Teach for America and change everything about her life.

Ms. Reid was an atypical TFA recruit. Everybody else was 21 and single and about to embark on their first professional adventure. She was 24 and married and an ex-federal employee. But she soon realized her initial work experience didn't give her a leg up for the road ahead. It was one thing to know a lot about math; teaching it was a whole different matter.

She got placed at a school in Baltimore—and as the first day of school approached, Ms. Reid realized how unprepared she felt. Unlike some of her colleagues, however, she'd never expected TFA to prepare her. In her mind, it was a simple transactional equation: she wanted a job, and once she got it, she'd take care of the rest herself.

Over the course of her first year, though, Ms. Reid came to feel differently. It was a crime she'd been placed in front of such beautiful, needy kids. They needed so many things, not least of which was learning to read, and she was not the best person for that job.

To plug the gaps in her own understanding, Ms. Reid read everything she could about literacy, and about how to teach phonics; and, gradually, she taught herself how to help her students learn.

In retrospect, they were the best teaching years of her life. She taught reading through social studies content—and tailored the content to the issues that were most relevant to her students. Hers was a classroom of Black and Brown faces, so Ms. Reid's students explored almost everything through the eyes of slaves or Native Americans. As she witnessed the ways in which her children became familiar with their own history, Ms. Reid felt the euphoria of discovering her calling in life.

Over the next five years she taught in several different charter schools, and fell in love with the freedom they provided and the innovation they unleashed around what a school can and should look like.

Then she heard the stark rhetoric of Michelle Rhee, and she felt drawn to the possibility of helping reform D.C.'s public school system.

Ms. Reid had never heard someone call it like it was so fearlessly. Up to that point, like a lot of people, she didn't believe meaningful change could come to an urban school district. Then, rather suddenly, she believed she had a responsibility to be a part of it. In 2009, she became Bancroft's first new principal in 20 years.

Three years later, Ms. Reid felt very differently. Rhee was no longer in charge of the city's schools, and Reid was no longer certain that the former Chancellor's tough rhetoric had helped her ability to do her job. It had been thrilling to hear someone coming in saying, "Let's kick some ass!" And yet Ms. Reid's brief tenure as principal had already shown her that meaningful change was a lot more complicated, and a lot less linear, in reality. A school is its people, she realized, not merely the data points they produce, and a cut-throat climate of the sort Rhee had created made it a lot harder to find and grow the people that could help her make Bancroft a transformational place. This was her make-or-break year.

The next morning, Ms. Reid paused briefly outside the door of room 121 to check in on two of her most promising teachers. She watched as Harvey entered the classroom, hung up his jacket, and sat down at his table to eat the free breakfast provided by the city to its school-children—on this day, an egg burrito, banana, and milk. Ms. Schmidt asked for volunteers to read the morning message.

Rodger raised his hand, and the other children's reactions let Ms. Reid know it was a significant event. Thus far he'd spoken fewer than 20 words out loud all year. But on this day he hesitantly approached the front of the room, placed a hand on his teacher's knee and squinted through thick glasses at the message he could barely read.

Harvey stared out the window as Ms. Schmidt read the message out loud, piece by piece. Rodger listened intently and repeated it back to her, like a vow.

## CHAPTER THREE

# The Known World

◇  ◇  ◇  **MV**  ◇  ◇  ◇

EVERY DAY AT 11 A.M., Mundo Verde's kindergartners would file out of their classrooms, into the city, and over to a nearby park for recess.

The park itself was one of D.C.'s most beautiful—filled with twisty slides and tunnels and large patches of manicured grass. But the journey there and back was the most stressful part of Berenice Pernalete's workday.

*Uno minutos ma-ás*, she sang to the children one morning while slipping on a yellow crossing guard vest and grabbing a bright orange flag. Teams of students shuttled back and forth between the bathrooms while others finished cleaning up refuse from the mid-morning snack.

By 11:10 A.M., the kindergartners had descended the long stairwell of the school to reach street level. Ms. Berenice and her co-teacher, Ms. Laura, shouted instructions at the children in Spanish and tried to move the herd at a steady pace. Two students held open the front door while the rest of their classmates poured out like liquid—formless and fast moving.

"*¡Bruno, la mano!*"

"*¡Jimmy, camina como un niño de Kinder!*"

Gradually, the pointillist painting of bodies before her settled into a clear line of children walking in pairs. Berenice and Laura led them along the edge of Florida Avenue—once known as Boundary Street when, long ago, it marked the literal edge of the city. Jimmy nearly tripped over his untied shoelaces, and Berenice bent down to help him. The other students sang or chatted patiently, blissfully unaware of the potential disasters that lay ahead.

*"¡Vamos, vamos, vamos! ¡Caminando rápido, sin correr!"*

The class reached the intersection of Florida and Connecticut Avenues, and Berenice scanned the streets for danger. Metro buses whizzed by, alongside delivery trucks, bicyclists, and mid-morning commuters. She waited for the walk sign to appear. When it did, she had 30 seconds to get everyone across before the six lanes of traffic resumed their routes into and out of the city center.

Berenice walked backward across the busy thoroughfare, making sure no one strayed off course and exhorting everyone to move at a steady pace. Most days, they made it with a second or two to spare. Some days, there would still be stragglers in the crosswalk—their teachers forming a human shield between them and the idling cars. No one seemed to mind; the motorists would sit and smile as they watched two or three adults try to corral 46 meandering children. But Berenice felt tense from the moment they left the school until the moment she got every child across the avenue and headed up the quiet side street, past the towering ambassadorial residences and private mansions, to the park.

As a teacher in a first-year charter school, Berenice's daily crossing of Connecticut Avenue was an unavoidable part of the job description. It would take several more years until Mundo Verde reached its full enrollment, which meant it would be several years before it could inhabit a more traditional "school" space. In the meantime, the newest schools had to make do with the city's other available resources to give their kids time to run and play. And in a city center like Dupont Circle, Mundo Verde only had one playground to choose from.

One mid-October morning, while the children played and she sat on one of the park's bright red benches, Berenice was finally in a position to relax. She watched her students' small bodies—still new to her—hang from the monkey bars or furtively huddle near immaculate hedges. A few gravitated toward her to exchange a quick greeting and then spun away again, like atoms. Almost always, the children spoke to their Spanish teacher in English. And always, Berenice spoke back in Spanish.

*"Para, mira y escucha,"* she sang to the children. Time to go. She unfurled the orange flag—her matador's cape—and watched as the children slowly lined up for the return trip to school.

◇  ◇  ◇  **B**  ◇  ◇  ◇

Rebecca Schmidt and Rebecca Lebowitz led their third-graders past the fire station on Newton Street, watching closely to make sure everyone made the turn onto 14th Street and toward the Columbia Heights Metro. Today was the day they were going to explore the history of the city and its monuments, but before the fun could commence, Ms. Lebowitz and Ms. Schmidt had to make sure no one got lost amid the bustle of the morning commute. The students' voices echoed off the concrete walls of the fire station, while their teachers shuttled back and forth along the long winding line, urging some to slow down and others to speed up.

The path they followed from the school to the Metro had no tour guide, but there was plenty of local history to discuss. For decades, 14th Street had served as an unofficial dividing line of the city after residents burned it to the ground in spontaneous outrage following the assassination of Martin Luther King in 1968. Since that day, it was well known that to the west lay the neighborhoods of privilege and power. To the east lay the neighborhoods of the poor. And all along 14th Street itself lay the hookers, the liquor stores, and the drug dealers.

Beginning in 2000, however, the street started to change. A 60,000 square-foot Whole Foods grocery store opened on the corner of 14th and P. Trendy bars and restaurants followed, first slowly and then in an entrepreneurial flood. New apartment buildings sprouted up on previously abandoned lots. And by the time the Two Rebeccas led their students down the escalator of the station and onto the subway cars, the changes had migrated far enough north to begin reshaping the neighborhoods that fed into Bancroft Elementary School.

By 2011, those neighborhoods—Columbia Heights, Mount Pleasant, Pleasant Plains, and Park View—were among the fastest gentrifying places in the United States. In the span of a decade, the White population had more than doubled—from 22% to 46%[1]—making it one of the more diverse areas of the city. The changes meant more than shifting demographics at Bancroft. They also meant that more and more new schools were opening in the area, all trying to meet the demand of families who wanted better educational options—and who still preferred, if possible, to keep their children close to home.

It was a curious feature of school choice in D.C., as a 2012 report commissioned by Mayor Vincent Gray made clear. "Despite the range of choices in the District," its authors wrote, "two-thirds of students attend a school within or adjacent to their neighborhood cluster. The pattern suggests that most students prefer to attend a school close to their home, [even though] for most students, a local performing school is not an option."[2]

Rebecca Lebowitz could have predicted its findings. Over the past three years she'd watched the youngest students at Bancroft become noticeably Whiter. It was almost, she said, as if her struggling school was starting to seem posh.

That certainly wasn't true in the older grades, where the students were still disproportionately Black and Brown. But Ms. Lebowitz worried about the ways Bancroft would be forced to adapt if the surrounding neighborhoods continued along their gentrifying path. A lot of Bancroft's extra services were supported by the federal funding it received because a majority of its students came from low-income families. What would happen if that funding went away? And what if all the new charter schools moving in ended up siphoning away too many of its students?

Ms. Lebowitz was not a fan of charter schools; she thought they privileged certain families over others and damaged the public system as a whole. She also wasn't sure how she could best contribute to making that system better for everyone; she just knew that she wanted to. These were big policy decisions that were going to have to be made by *someone*. Why not someone like her?

That thought was what drew her to start considering graduate school; and that idea had only grown in her mind since the end of the summer and the start to the year. By the fall, Ms. Lebowitz was spending most evenings on the couch in her apartment, working on her personal statement while her roommates watched sports on TV, and trying to decide exactly what she wanted for herself and her future.

"I was raised on a word farm in Newton, Massachusetts," her essay began. "Actually, my parents aren't really farmers; they are educators who believe that language and literacy are the nitrogen of learning. Growing up in this environment of ceaseless and open-minded reading and conversation, I came to appreciate diverse points of view. And in the process I have developed a commitment to multicultural, social-justice-based education. Now, after three years as a Teaching Fellow in an underperforming school in Washington, D.C. I am applying for a master's degree program at Harvard in order to explore best practices in teaching, to learn leadership skills, and to understand more deeply how policy decisions affect school performance."

The subway arrived at the Smithsonian station, and the students bunched up on the escalators while bemused commuters squeezed by. Ms. Lebowitz and Ms. Schmidt took the stairs to sprint past them—stacks of green Metro passes thick like cards in their hands.

First stop, the National Mall.

What is the ultimate purpose of a city? What are its special responsibilities and its unique powers? And what does it promise to the people who choose to live there?

For generations, policymakers have been asking those questions in an effort to improve the quality of our urban institutions and resources. Innovations in areas such as housing, transportation, and public works have helped fuel significant rises in the populations of major American cities after decades of decline. Until recently, however, most Americans witnessed few structural changes to what is arguably a city's most valuable institution: its public school system.

No one would have dared to predict such sustained inactivity would be possible back in 1954, after Thurgood Marshall's historic victory in *Brown v. Board of Education,* the U.S. Supreme Court decision that triumphantly reaffirmed a core American principle: "In the field of public education the doctrine of 'separate but equal' has no place." Yet if Marshall were alive today, he would urge us to stop celebrating the symbolic victory of *Brown*, and start accepting our actual responsibility for tolerating a public education system that is, clearly, still separate, and still unequal.

Marshall said so himself, in a lesser known 1973 Court opinion, *San Antonio v. Rodriguez.* By then he was no longer the lead lawyer arguing the case; he was the Court's first African American justice, issuing a ruling. And this time, he was on the losing side.

The case began when a group of poor Texas parents claimed that their state's tolerance of the wide disparity in school resources—which were, like the rest of the country, primarily determined by property taxes—violated the Equal Protection Clause of the 14th Amendment.[3] A state court agreed, but the U.S. Supreme Court, in a narrow 5–4 decision, reversed.

Gone from the Court's 1973 ruling was its 1954 contention that "education is perhaps the most important function of state and local governments." Gone, too, was its assertion that "it is doubtful any child may reasonably be expected to succeed in life if he is denied the opportunity of an education. Such an opportunity," wrote a unanimous Court in *Brown*, "where the state has undertaken to provide it, is a right which must be made available to all on equal terms."[4]

Instead, the five-justice majority in *Rodriguez* wrote simply that while the Texas school system's approach to funding "can fairly be described as chaotic and unjust . . . it does not follow that this system violates the Constitution. Though education is one of the most important services performed by the state, it is not within the limited category of rights recognized by this Court as guaranteed by the Constitution." If it were, the majority conceded, "virtually every State will not pass muster."[5]

For Justice Marshall, that was precisely the point. "The Court concludes that public education is not constitutionally guaranteed," he wrote, even though "no other state function is so uniformly recognized as an essential element of our society's well being."

For Marshall, American democracy couldn't work without a guarantee of equal access to a high-quality public education. "Education directly affects the ability of a child to exercise his First Amendment rights," he explained. "Education prepares individuals to be self-reliant and self-sufficient participants in society. Both facets of this observation are suggestive of the substantial relationship which education bears to guarantees of our Constitution."

Marshall's passionate beliefs notwithstanding, by the start of the 2011–2012 school year, the issues he'd raised in his *Rodriguez* dissent remained unaddressed in most communities across the country. Public schools were still largely funded by local property taxes; one out of every five American children was living in poverty; and massive spending disparities remained between schools. In other words, a desirable five-digit zip code was still, in most places, the surest lottery ticket to a better future.

In recent years, however, the intractable destiny of one's zip code was starting to change in cities across the United States as a result of the growth of the school choice movement, and, in particular, the growth of public charter schools.

Originally conceived of as autonomous public schools, the idea was that in exchange for maintaining a commitment to educate all children, charter schools would be freed to think more innovatively about issues like governance, curriculum, budgeting, staffing, and the school calendar. The first public charter school law was passed in Minnesota in 1991, and today, almost every state in the nation has one—including D.C. By 2012, D.C. had more students enrolled in charter schools than almost any city in the country: across 57 schools in all, and serving nearly half of the students in the city.

For educators, parents, and policymakers across the country, the question was whether school choice was moving cities closer to, or further from, Thurgood Marshall's vision of a more equitable and high-functioning public school system. And even in D.C., a city that had been experimenting with school choice for more than a decade, it was too soon to tell.

Supporters argue that more choice in the marketplace will not only motivate parents like never before, but also unleash new ideas about teaching and learning that can be shared to help all schools improve. Critics claim school choice is merely creating another tier in an unequal system in which motivated middle- and working-class parents can find more desirable options for their children, leaving the unlucky and the unmotivated behind in the increasingly undesirable neighborhood schools that remain.

At Mundo Verde and Bancroft, opinions were split. Whereas Rebecca Lebowitz believed charter schools would weaken public schools overall, Rebecca Schmidt was open to the idea of working at one. And whereas Zakiya Reid began her career at a charter school, she'd made a conscious decision to work for the district. By contrast, Dahlia Aguilar had left her position at a neighborhood school to help start Mundo Verde from scratch.

Even Kristin Scotchmer, who turned her whole life upside down by quitting her job to become Mundo Verde's inaugural executive director, felt torn. "How do we create a virtuous cycle of sustainability between charter schools and district schools?" she wondered one afternoon at a coffee shop near the school. "I don't think anyone has figured that out yet, and I've learned it's unavoidable sometimes to feel messed up about the way some of this stuff unfolds. We got a lot of our desks and materials from three other charter schools that are being closed. That felt bizarre. But it's also a reflection of the clarity of each school's plan, and the sort of creative destruction that the current environment allows. Those schools invested a lot of their money recklessly, in high-quality physical resources. Then they didn't meet their enrollment targets, and the next thing you know they'd lost control of their own vision.

"The biggest thing I worry about," she confessed, "is whether charter schools will find ways to work collaboratively with other public schools in the city, and not merely be a siphon for the most motivated families. Public schools have to serve the public good. If they don't, what happens to our shared commitment to justice for all? And what happens to the city as a whole? What does its overriding purpose become?"

Long before citizens like Kristin Scotchmer began to wrestle with the question of a city's purpose, and long before there was ever an idea like school choice, a man named Lewis Mumford spent his entire career researching the unique role of cities in the evolution of modern civilization. His 1961 tome, *The City in History*, is considered one of the most important books ever written on the subject.

For Mumford, the search for answers begins as far back as our collective memory can take us—"in the rites of the cave," where humankind first experienced "the social and religious impulses that conspired to draw men finally into cities, where all the original feelings of awe, reverence, pride, and joy would be further magnified by art, and multiplied by the number of responsive participants."[6] These earliest ancient sanctuaries, Mumford believed, were the places that seeded the first hints of civic life, of shared responsibility, and of a true collective identity. "Beginning as a representation of the cosmos, a means of bringing heaven down to earth, the city became a symbol of the possible. Utopia was an integral part of its original constitution, and precisely because it took form as an ideal projection, it brought into existence realities that might have remained latent for an indefinite time in more soberly governed small communities, pitched to lower expectations and unwilling to make exertions that transcended both their workaday habits and their mundane hopes."[7]

The *promise* of the city, in other words, preceded its actual existence. We have always been drawn to one another by the lure of co-creating more valuable and meaningful lives, Mumford argued. "Thus even before the city is a place of fixed residence, it begins as a meeting place to which people periodically return: the magnet comes before the container, and this ability to attract non-residents to it for intercourse and spiritual stimulus no less than trade remains one of the essential criteria of the city, a witness to its inherent dynamism, as opposed to the more fixed and indrawn form of the village, hostile to the outsider."[8]

Other urban historians agree, such as Jane Jacobs, author of the equally celebrated *The Death and Life of Great American Cities*: "Lively, diverse, intense cities contain the seeds of their own regeneration," Jacobs wrote, "with energy enough to carry over for problems and needs outside themselves."[9]

Over the course of its history, Washington, D.C. had repeatedly proven to be in need of its own seeds of regeneration. Burned to the ground by the British in the War of 1812, savaged by the crack epidemic of the 1980s, the national capital was first proposed as an idea back in 1790, when Congress passed the Residence Act and authorized President George Washington to place a district of 100 square miles—10 by 10—somewhere along the Potomac River.

Washington liked the idea for a few reasons; it would be within riding distance of his beloved home in Mount Vernon; and, more important, it would rest halfway between northernmost Maine and southernmost Georgia. No state would have jurisdiction over the territory, and, best of all, it could be designed from scratch—a world-wonder that would house the government of the world's next great empire.

To design such a place, Washington turned to a thirty-something ex-Frenchman named Pierre L'Enfant. Talented and ambitious, L'Enfant was already well-known for designing Federal Hall in New York City. Washington tasked him with surveying the land and sketching out a proposal. L'Enfant not only did so; he provided an accompanying memorandum in which he outlined in great detail a vision far exceeding anything Washington had imagined up to that point.

This would not just be some city sprouting up along a small patch of the Potomac, L'Enfant explained; it would incorporate every square inch of those 100 square miles—making it 15 times the size of any city Washington had ever visited. As one scholar noted, "L'Enfant's desire to write something magnificent across the land was helping Washington to see his way up and out of a fog of provincialism and into the clearer air, where he could launch a capital truly worthy of the country. It was a dramatic shift in perspective, sidelining the local in favor of the national, the present in favor of the future, and the familiar in favor of the extraordinary."[10]

Unfortunately, L'Enfant's grandness of vision was commensurate with a grandness of self, and it didn't take long before his bombast alienated several people essential to the project's completion—including Thomas Jefferson. Nonetheless, many of the original ideas he had for the city—wide diagonal avenues, distinct neighborhoods, and a "Grand Avenue" lined by public gardens—carried over, even if he could no longer lead the construction itself. Indeed, although L'Enfant's own story ends tragically—he died in poverty, convinced his vision for D.C. would die with him—his Grand Avenue survives by another name: The National Mall.

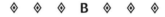

As Bancroft's third-graders skipped along the walkways that lined the grassy patches of the Mall, their Ethiopian tour guide, a friendly middle-aged man named Mengistu, provided a running narration of what they were seeing. "The word 'Mall' means gathering place," he shouted; a few students, like Elliott, listened closely, while others jostled, whispered, or jumped. "And this is the gathering place for all the people in the country."

The group slowly walked toward the Capitol, and most of the children stayed together in a tight cluster around Mengistu; two, however, marked opposite poles—Lourdes, who ran far ahead, forcing Ms. Schmidt to keep up; and Harvey, who lagged far behind to jump up on each passing park bench and practice his karate kicks, forcing Ms. Lebowitz to fall back and urge him forward. Harvey picked up a few of the fallen leaves around him. "This one is dead! This one is alive!" he exclaimed. Ms. Lebowitz smiled and nodded in affirmation as they reached the small reflecting pool in front of the Capitol, where Elliott's shrieks could be heard: "I see the water!"

Lourdes had already begun sprinting up Capitol Hill. Small and slight, with dark brown skin, brown eyes, and long black hair, Lourdes had become a student of interest for Ms. Schmidt. One of four children, she had two older sisters; both had passed through room 121 in previous years, and both were high-functioning, hardworking students. But Lourdes and her younger brother were born during a period of their mother's life when she was struggling with an addiction to drugs. As a result, both suffered from similar comprehension and language delays.

Ms. Schmidt noticed that in addition to her learning challenges, Lourdes was a fiery, stubborn spirit who took a long time to trust people. Already, they'd learned the futility of telling Lourdes to do something; she would just do the opposite. Ms. Schmidt knew from past experiences that the key to being successful with a child like Lourdes was to find a way to earn her trust and make her feel safe. That was made more challenging by the fact that daily lessons in reading and math didn't play to Lourdes's strengths; that was reserved for the athletic field, where despite her small stature, she was both the fastest and the best soccer player in the grade—boys included.

Ms. Schmidt did her best to scamper up the hill after her. Lourdes sat down near the base of the Capitol dome, waiting to be punished. Instead Ms. Schmidt crouched next to her and dabbed at the tight beads of perspiration on her forehead. "How long you think it will take the rest of them to reach us?" she asked. Lourdes broke into a wide smile.

◊  ◊  ◊  **MV**  ◊  ◊  ◊

The cramped rectangular room that served as Mundo Verde's conference space filled slowly with tired teachers, while outside its door the daily pickup filled the *Zocalo* with the energetic voices of reuniting children and parents. It was mid-afternoon but most of the teachers had still not eaten lunch; the room smelled of homemade sandwiches and salads. Berenice Pernalete found a chair near the edge of the room and took a sip from her water bottle to quench her parched mouth—the result of five straight hours of talking and interacting without a break.

The focus of that day's professional development was one Berenice was particularly eager to learn more about: student expeditions. Like the rest of the faculty, she'd never actually seen one, let alone designed one herself, so it was a mixture of curiosity and anxiety she felt as she waited for Romey Pittman to arrive.

Romey was the school designer who worked for Expeditionary Learning, a national network of schools that developed out of an unlikely partnership between the founders of Outward Bound and the faculty of Harvard's Graduate School of Education. For decades, Outward Bound had provided adults and young people with challenging outdoor wilderness courses. Over the same period, Harvard's faculty had been busy investigating what sorts of places could best support learning and growth. In 1987, the two sides came together when they realized they had reached the same conclusion via very different paths: that the best possible learning environment is one that is hands-on, challenging, and relationship-rich—and that if we were serious about helping young people learn to use their minds well, we should start designing schools with those core principles in mind.

By 2011, the partnership had grown into a network of hundreds of schools across the country. Each school pledged to embody the Design Principles of Expeditionary Learning, while the network pledged to honor the different ways each school might go about embodying those principles. The connective tissue between the network and its members was made up of people like Romey, who helped shape the professional development calendars of the schools in her region, and who also provided ongoing mentoring and support.

Romey opened the door of the conference room and offered a welcoming grin. Her tightly curled hair sprang out in playful angles, and wrinkles formed around her eyes that reflected a life of smiling. She carried with her a large canvas colorfully decorated with words and pictures. "This is a documentation panel," she began. "I brought it in because I want us to imagine what our expeditions are going to look like when we've finished them and invite everyone's families to see the amazing work their children completed."

Berenice scanned the board, which another school had covered with background information, pictures, artifacts, and guiding questions. "See if the panel helps you understand the goals of this particular expedition," Romey instructed, "and if it explains what it was the students set out to discover. A good expedition is like a knowledge treasure hunt. It takes children out of their classrooms, into the community, and through a vigorous process that turns them into experts on a subject they want to know more about."

Romey took out a stack of photographs documenting different stages of different schools' expeditions and passed them around. "As you look at these, what do you notice? Can you tell what each expedition's core components were? Can you guess what the guiding question might have been?"

Berenice stared at each picture. The faces of the adults and children radiated deep satisfaction in what they had done together, and the work itself—whether it was a series of scientific drawings, a municipal proposal, or a visual explanation of a tested hypothesis—was of a quality Berenice had never seen before. This is beyond worksheets, she thought. This is *craftsmanship*. As Romey broke the faculty into grade-specific teams—as an Expeditionary Learning school, Mundo Verde hoped to organize one expedition each semester in every grade—Berenice felt a renewed sense of gratitude for the profession she had chosen.

It was ironic, since she'd become a teacher for all the wrong reasons. Berenice's plan was to return to Venezuela after graduating from LSU. Her father told her she was crazy. You'd be a fool to come back, he said. I heard they're issuing visas for teachers. Try it for a year while you figure everything else out.

Berenice felt insulted at the thought. I went to school for four years just to teach the ABCs? Then she took the summer crash course to get certified, and she felt even worse; it seemed like they were just giving certifications away. By the time she started working at an elementary school on the outskirts of Houston, Berenice could not have felt worse about her first job.

Then she met her students, and she got to know their families. "I would encounter these struggling Mexican ladies and families that really needed someone, and it broke my heart to see how they struggled so much to get here," she said. "They would share their stories with me. They needed help to translate the electricity bill. And they didn't feel safe with anyone but their kid's teacher."

The school was obsessed with making sure its Spanish-speaking students learned English as soon as possible, but Berenice offered them different advice. "I was telling them you have to keep speaking Spanish. Being bilingual would give them a better shot at life. That was my guerilla work."

As Berenice and Molly sat down to think about the expedition, they settled in on something that would be both interesting and reflective of the school's commitment to sustainability. "What if the guiding question was something like, 'Where does the water we use come from, and where does it go after we use it?'" Molly suggested.

"Yes!" Berenice shouted back. "We could have them do some fact-finding at the hotel across the street and find out from the staff how much water is used. Maybe the final project could be a product that helped hotel guests become more aware of the importance of water conservation."

Molly and Berenice continued to plan, excited at the chance to craft a sustained and active learning experience—and worried about how they would find the time to do it, given everything else that was already underway. Mundo Verde's original application to the D.C. Public Charter School Board had been one of the most thorough ever submitted—and one of the most ambitious. Not just an Expeditionary Learning school, not just a language immersion school, and not just a school committed to sustainability, Mundo Verde aspired to be all three things, and to do them all equally well. Meanwhile, the first report cards were due in a few weeks—and no one was sure what the format would be. They still hadn't completed the initial literacy and numeracy assessments of every kid to establish their baseline data of what each child knew before the school year began. And they already had a limited amount of class time to begin with. What was the right balance between the school's commitment to advance its kindergartners' reading, writing, and math skills, and its determination to make learning come alive?

"I don't know how we're going to do all these things well," Molly confessed as she packed up her bag and prepared to head home.

"I know," Berenice added, "we need to give this project a real WOW factor for the parents when it's all done."

"*And* we need to teach their kids to read."

Bancroft's third-graders patrolled the walls surrounding the chiseled sculpture of Martin Luther King, oblivious to the words that were carved there. Ms. Lebowitz shuffled alongside them, reading each quote one by one.

> *The arc of the moral universe is long, but it bends toward justice.*
>
> *We are caught in an inescapable network of mutuality, tied in a single garment of destiny.*
>
> *Make a career of humanity. Commit to the noble struggle for equal rights. You will make a greater person of yourself, a greater nation of your country, and a finer world to live in.*
>
> *True peace is not merely the absence of tension; it is the presence of justice.*

She wanted to keep reading, but the students had begun a large—and inappropriate—game of tag. She looked down to find Lourdes by her side. "Missus, did you know the new *Transformers* movie was filmed here?" she asked excitedly. "I did not know that," her teacher responded. "Help me gather everyone else up and back on the bus."

As they pulled out of the parking lot, Ms. Lebowitz and Ms. Schmidt checked the time. Could they drive by the White House on the way back to school? they asked Mengistu. Of course, he said.

The class bounced along the southern edge of 14th Street, past the Washington Monument on one side and the Capitol building on the other. The students' gazes, however, were pointed inside the bus and toward each other, the result of a spirited discussion that had broken out around what different people were going to be for Halloween.

"I'm going to be a shadow icewolf ninja," said Harvey.

"I'm going to be a witch," Lourdes added.

"I don't celebrate Halloween," said Francesca. "We're Adventists."

"Well, those of you that do go better remember to bring a jacket or a sweater," Ms. Lebowitz added while Ms. Schmidt sat next to her, lost in her own thoughts. It had been a long day, with stops at the Mall, the Jefferson, Lincoln, King, and FDR Memorials, and now a final drive past what L'Enfant had once referred to simply as the "President's House."

The bus neared its turn toward McPherson Square, and most of the Halloween conversations stopped. The students kneeled on their seats to get a better look at the White House, wondering out loud if they were going to see President Obama or, better yet, his dog Bo.

Ms. Schmidt looked in the other direction. It was only a month old, but already the Occupy movement that began in Manhattan had started to ricochet around the world, including D.C. Right there, in the shadow of the White House, a crowded tent city had sprung up in a public park. Just like the Hoovervilles of the 1930s, she thought—a physical reminder of the injustices in our midst, and the need of the people to fight against them.

The bus slowed as the students spotted sharpshooters on the White House roof—"I see a gun!" Elliott shouted. Then it made its final turn up 14th Street and back in the direction of the school. Ms. Schmidt watched as three residents of the nascent tent city talked animatedly just off the grass of McPherson Square, next to a sign welcoming all to The People's Library.

A young boy with wild hair and colorful clothes—younger than her students, no doubt the tent city's youngest resident—rode his tricycle directly into a stream of busy midday commuters. Ms. Schmidt watched as he disappeared amidst the beige and blue crush of business attire.

Then the boy circled back, weaving his way through the foot traffic to re-enter his city within a city. The strangers surrounding him shifted their strides to let him pass without ever looking down to see him, and the boy, squarely focused on the family in front of him, never felt the need to look up.

## CHAPTER FOUR

# What I See

◇  ◇  ◇  **B**  ◇  ◇  ◇

EVERY DAY, AMIDST the quotidian pull of meetings, emergencies, and budgetary crises, Zakiya Reid reserved at least an hour for walking the halls of her school. And every week, she tried to visit each of her school's 30 classrooms at least once.

Because Bancroft was first built in the 1920s, the school Ms. Reid patrolled would feel familiar to almost any student of the past century: the hallways were comfortably wide, the floors an archetypal checkerboard pattern of green and white tiles, and the ceilings exposed patchworks of black pipes, red valves, and fluorescent lights. And because Bancroft was originally built to accommodate the children of a rapidly growing section of the city, the classrooms she visited were almost all spacious and airy, with high ceilings, large windows, and familiar aesthetic trappings: wall clocks (several of which were broken), wall maps (many of which were out of date), and distinct tuckaway corners for student lockers and cubbies.

Twice a year, Ms. Reid's casual surveying of her school became more formal as part of the city's controversial new teacher evaluation system, IMPACT. First implemented during Michelle Rhee's tenure, IMPACT had initiated a degree of specificity and formality that felt like a far cry from the previous era, when almost every teacher was rated "effective," and when most observations were conducted informally. Now, principals like Ms. Reid were expected to spend up to 30 minutes every few months observing their teachers and rating them across nine distinct categories.

For many of Bancroft's teachers, particularly veterans with the clearest frame of reference to an alternative, IMPACT felt cold and impersonal—a slapdash effort to take a profession that was pure art and recast it as pure science. Conventional wisdom had always held that it was impossible to measure the effectiveness of a teacher—that it was too wrapped up in the relationships, the real-time decisions, and the myriad social, intellectual, and emotional realities on the ground. For many, IMPACT seemed to be suggesting the opposite— that not only can a teacher's overall effectiveness be measured, it can be reduced to a single score, and that those scores can then determine everything from who gets hired and fired to who deserves the biggest year-end bonus. Indeed, it was now possible for individual teachers in DCPS to make as much as $25,000 in bonuses each year. For many, however, the promise of more money was negated by the fear of less autonomy. And so, on a cold early December morning when Ms. Reid arrived for a day of IMPACT observations, she braced herself for the resistance she expected to encounter.

It had been a difficult semester thus far. Aside from the baby inside her that was making her joints ache and her ankles swell, Ms. Reid could tell that morale among her teachers was low. Many of them were being asked to do something very different from what they'd done their whole careers, and many remained convinced that the essence of what they did was simply too unique to be streamlined. For these educators, IMPACT wasn't feedback; it was an eviction notice. And in those situations, Ms. Reid wasn't sure how to shift that perception—or, in some cases, if she even wanted to.

The full range of challenges was on display by mid-morning, as she sat in the back of a second-grade classroom. A mixture of anger and frustration rose inside her as she watched a teacher struggle to explain a lesson clearly to her students. The teacher was clearly hardworking and dedicated to her kids. She also wasn't very good at helping them learn. Ms. Reid watched as she facilitated a small group of students through a literature lesson from behind her half-moon desk. While the rest of the class wrote silently at their desks, the teacher, dressed in a yellow Bancroft T-shirt, asked the four students in front of her to read different passages of the story, to make predictions of what would happen next, and then to consider which "schema" the author was working from.

Ms. Reid took notes on her iPad. "Confusing vocabulary choices." "Out of step developmentally with the children's needs." "Questions too leading." "Too much teacher talk." By the time the 30-minute observation was concluded, the same four students sat in front of the teacher's desk, and there had been no interaction with any of the other students in the room. Near the door, one boy squirmed in a silent agony of boredom as he watched his principal get up to leave.

Ms. Reid felt helpless when she considered situations like the one she'd just observed—helpless to show the teacher how to improve her practice, and helpless to do anything about the fact that 30 of Bancroft's second-graders were being lulled to sleep on a daily basis. "Sometimes I long for the charter environment," Reid confessed as she made her way downstairs for the next observation. "Just the thought of being able to build your own staff. Here I'm coming in and in some cases trying to get people to reverse practices they've been doing for 20 years. No one likes to feel like they're no good at what they do. But differentiated instruction is not just different activities—it's different plans for different kids. This is a very different profession now, and it *needs* to be. We all need to change."

By December, Molly Howard was desperate for the sort of detailed feedback Zakiya Reid was trying to provide—and increasingly frustrated that she wasn't receiving it.

"Threeee moooore minutes!" she sang one morning as the students finished up their breakfasts—cereal, an apple, and some milk. "Threeee moooore minutes!" they sang back to her.

Molly hit the chime at her desk, and the students crossed their arms. "OK friends, it's that time of day. Time to stop, clean up, and come to the carpet."

As the winter break drew nearer, Molly had found a way to keep the chaotic energy of the Zebras at bay. Some of the improvement was due to changes that occurred outside the classroom—since the school's meeting with his mom, for example, Albert had become a much calmer classmate, no doubt due in large part to the fact that he was finally getting enough sleep. But most of the changes were due to Molly's relentless brand of energy, her commitment to get better, and her ability to establish clear boundaries, rituals, and expectations for the group.

The familiar transition between breakfast and carpet time was one example. So was the initial set of activities the children did together, like the question of the morning. On this day, Molly had written a question on butcher paper at the front of the room: *What would you rather be: a pilot or a police person?* She let every student vote and explain their choice, and then asked a volunteer to count up the tallies. Then the class stood and played an interactive game. A favorite involved one student at a time weaving throughout the circle and looking for a partner to pull into the center, while the rest of the class held hands and sang, "Bluebird, Bluebird, through my window—Oh Johnny I am tired. Pick a partner and hop in the gar-den." In the past, a game like this was an opportunity for Albert to punch someone; now he merely squealed with delight, relishing his increasing likelihood of being chosen to join someone in the center. And every student seemed grateful for the predictability of the day's schedule and sequence of events.

The consistency of the daily rhythm was very much by design, a reflection of Molly's understanding that minds seek patterns, particularly young minds. In fact, all human beings seek "patternicity"—the effort to find structure even when there is none. As neuroscientist David Eagleman explains it, "perception works not by building up bits of captured data, but instead by matching *expectations* to incoming sensory data." In other words, "our expectations influence what we see."[1] And Molly had learned from experience that the less her students' brains were left in a state of fear or anxiety or uncertainty about what to expect, the more she could expect them to act safely, listen carefully, and be fully present.

Still, there was so much more to learn, and so many ways to get better. As Molly led the Zebras through their morning activities and toward the part of the day when they would work more concretely on reading and writing skills, she watched the door, wondering if anyone would be visiting today to observe her.

It stayed shut. She silently boiled. The distinction between good and very good teachers is not very big—but the leap to great is exponential. And there was no way she'd ever be great if she kept having to figure out everything for herself.

Since she'd decided to become a teacher, Molly had been searching for a mentor she could learn from—and repeatedly come up empty. Her initial training was a yearlong residency in a high-performing charter school in D.C. The year she spent in residence, however, was also the school's first year in a new building, and Molly felt lost amidst a school-wide shuffle of non-curricular concerns. Even her past experience in the private sector had left her looking for feedback and receiving little, other than the generic praise for a "job well done." When she accepted the job at Mundo Verde, she'd hoped to find some sources of wisdom that could help her hone her craft.

Dahlia Aguilar was an ideal candidate to fill that role, with extensive experience, a nuanced understanding of pedagogy and how people learn, and a sharp determination to deepen her own understanding of early childhood. But Dahlia was also a first-time principal in a first-year school, and something she and Molly and everyone else had learned was the unique madness of navigating an inaugural semester when there are no systems in place to shape how decisions get made, how student growth gets tracked, and how problems get solved. For better or worse, everything needed to be built from scratch. And for better or worse, some things ended up getting more attention than others.

Teacher evaluation was not one of those things, at least not yet. Molly kneeled in front of a group of students to discuss the components of a good storyteller voice, right in front of the three large vertical windows that looked out on the townhouses and apartment buildings of 20th Street. The outline of her body formed a faint image in the windows' sunny glare, just enough to suggest the shape of a person to the foot traffic below.

They couldn't have known it, but young women like Molly had chosen to become teachers at perhaps the most difficult and exciting time in the history of American public education.

Since the polarizing tenure of Michelle Rhee in D.C., Americans across the country had been paying unprecedented amounts of attention to schools and teachers, and debating what it would take to ensure that every American classroom was staffed with a great one.

At the center of those debates were differing responses to a question we've been wrestling with since the legendary educator John Dewey first proposed it almost a century ago as *the* question adults need to help young people answer for themselves: *What does it mean to be free?*

Dewey had a very specific answer to that question that was meant to guide educators in their work—an answer we've been ignoring or misinterpreting ever since. And the reason teachers like Molly Howard and principals like Zakiya Reid were working in an unprecedented period of change is because American public education is in the midst of redefining what it means to be free for both teachers and students—and those answers are taking each group in *opposite directions.*

As recently as the late 1990s, for example, it was possible to be a teacher in a public school without being certified. (I should know; I was one.) It was possible to compose daily lessons without paying any attention to state standards (and, of course, national standards didn't exist). It was possible to believe that the only real expertise that was required to be a great teacher was in one's content area. And it was possible to go through an entire year without anyone else in the school having much of a sense, if any, of what you did in your classroom day in and day out.

Being a teacher, in other words, involved many freedoms and few structures. That's why for educators who'd lived and worked through that era, it felt (and not inaccurately so) like their profession was heading in the exact opposite direction. The art of teaching was being subsumed by the science of learning, and magic was being diminished by measurement. That was certainly the assumption Zakiya Reid encountered every time she stepped into a veteran educator's classroom to conduct a formal evaluation. And that was the assumption that led people like D.C. Schools Chancellor Kaya Henderson—Rhee's former deputy—to propose basing as much as 50% of a teacher's evaluation under IMPACT on student test scores.

The challenge was avoiding the lure of either extreme and finding a way to have the pendulum rest in the center—to leverage new understandings about the science of the brain and apply new methods of assessing student learning in ways that enhanced, not diminished, the art of great teaching. But as school leaders like Zakiya Reid and Dahlia

Aguilar discovered, it was awfully hard to do that amidst everything else that was happening in a school day to day, and almost impossible to do if policymakers and district leaders kept overvaluing a single data point—test scores—at the expense of nearly everything else.

Meanwhile, a similarly tectonic shift was happening with students. And in that case, the definition of what it means to be free was expanding, not constricting.

Think of it this way: almost every adult in America, no matter the age, has experienced a remarkably similar education. We were probably tracked into ability-grouped classes. We almost certainly sat in rows and spent the bulk of the school day listening as our teachers lectured. We received letter grades. And we understood that the job of the school was not to adjust to us; our job was to adjust to it.

For the bulk of this century, however, American public education has moved in the direction of trying to make learning more personalized and customized. And while that slow-developing shift is great news for students, it also makes the daily task of teaching a lot more challenging, resulting in a complete redefinition of the sorts of skills a great teacher should possess. Gone are the days where deep content knowledge is seen as the foundation of a teacher's professional expertise: now it is just as important to be fluent in cognitive science, child development, and a much more varied set of pedagogical strategies to employ throughout the year. And because these new definitions of teacher and student autonomy have outpaced most of the programs that prepare teachers for the classroom, most of today's educators are left, like Molly, to spend their evenings figuring it all out on the fly, while principals like Ms. Reid spend their days evaluating teachers based on a new framework that is much more specific, prescriptive, and high-stakes.

Ironically, some of the features of this "brave new world" of public education are similar to the vision John Dewey first proposed almost a century ago. As he put it, helping young people understand what it means to be free means helping them understand who they are and what they value—and that requires more than merely differentiating a daily lesson. "Since freedom resides in the operation of intelligent observation and judgment by which a purpose is developed," Dewey explained, "guidance given by the teacher to the exercise of the pupils' intelligence is an aid to freedom, not a restriction upon it."[2]

Learning what it means to be free, in other words, required the right balance of individual freedom and group structure, the right blend of student autonomy and adult guidance, and the right mixture of immeasurable art and measurable science. In fact, Dewey believed the ideal model for any school's approach to teaching and learning was the scientific method itself. That meant taking children, no matter the subject, on a six-step process of asking questions; conducting research; constructing a hypothesis; gathering information; analyzing data; and then adjusting one's understanding and behavior accordingly.

In Dewey's day, however, a word like "data" was still used in the spirit of its original Latin meaning: "something given." By contrast, in today's modern educational landscape, the word "data" has become a proxy for a single metric: student reading and math scores. That's why so many of Bancroft's most experienced teachers, either implicitly or explicitly, were pushing back against their young principal and her efforts to make the school more "data-driven." And it's why being a public school teacher in 2011–2012 was so exciting, and so challenging.

 ◊   ◊   ◊   **B**   ◊   ◊   ◊

By 1:00 P.M., Ms. Reid had one observation left to complete. She entered room 121 just as the students were returning from lunch. Ms. Lebowitz was giving a boy named Ernesto a sticker for taking his new ADD/ADHD medication when her principal entered the room. "Yesterday he passed out during drama class," Lebowitz explained as Ernesto walked away. "Apparently his medicine gets lost as he passes between his mom's and his dad's house. So we wanted to let him know that we've really noticed a difference in his behavior."

Ms. Reid sat in the back and watched as Ms. Lebowitz invited the class to the carpet to listen to a story. It was an incongruous site: all those nine-year-old bodies cramped together on the floor for story time, just as the earliest hints of their looming adolescence were starting to sprout.

Ms. Lebowitz started speaking, and Ms. Reid began taking notes. "Precise instructions." "Clearly defined goals." "Authoritative presence."

"Today we're on the lookout for words we don't recognize," Lebowitz explained over the hiss of the room's ancient radiator, "so we can practice making educated guesses about what they might mean by using context clues. As you listen to the story, be on the lookout for any words you don't know. And when you hear one, raise your hand."

Ms. Lebowitz began reading, and after a few paragraphs Lourdes raised her hand.

"What does 'Bubbelah' mean?"

"Great question. What do you think it means, based on the way it's being used? Talk to your neighbor, and try to support your answer by pointing to a clue in the story."

Ms. Reid listened to 30 young voices speaking simultaneously. *This* was what good instruction looked like. *This* was what an orderly classroom climate felt like. And this was how a school like hers could prepare young people to make sense of a world that was filled with unfamiliar words, customs, and expectations. As she looked down at her iPad, Ms. Reid found it easy to match a lot of what she was seeing in Ms. Lebowitz's lesson with the IMPACT categories: tying a lesson to specific content standards; explaining content clearly; checking for student understanding. And at the same time, she wondered if she and her colleagues were losing the capacity to see anything else.

That was the hardest part of being a public school principal—reconciling the belief, on one hand, that more precise and rigorous teacher evaluations were an essential part of school improvement; and accepting the reality, on the other hand, that tools like IMPACT were still very much imperfect works in progress, and that the Deweyesque reasons she got into teaching in the first place—to help kids discover who they are and what they value—weren't things she thought about that much anymore.

Molly Howard sat on her bed in her studio apartment and leaned over her laptop, drafting an outline of issues she wanted to raise with her bosses. It was already late, and she knew she needed to start slowing her brain down so she could sleep and save up the energy she'd need to make it through tomorrow. She also knew she couldn't wait another day—that if she didn't speak up and say something, this might be her one and only year at Mundo Verde.

"Major topics for conversation," Molly wrote across the top of the document, before listing four main areas of concern. "1. Next year. 2. Evaluation. 3. Support. 4. Communication." "What is the formalized process for evaluation?" she wrote. "Where is the regular form of communication? Where do we stand? Where are our breaks???"

The next morning, Molly spoke with Kristin and Dahlia while her students ate breakfast. "I know we're new," she began. "I'm proud of the work we've already accomplished as a team. But I need more feedback about my teaching, because I've realized that without more support I don't think I can sustain the energy required to do this job well. I'm starting to burn out, and it isn't even winter break."

"I know you guys need some structured time to catch your breath during the day," Dahlia said. "I've been feeling bad about that; it's pretty inhumane not to have breaks or planning time. We'll find a way to address that immediately."

Molly smiled cautiously as she left their office and returned to her classroom. Dahlia and Kristin looked at each other.

"Right when you think you're starting to figure it out!" Kristin said.

"She's right, obviously," Dahlia replied. "All of it. But I also think she and the other teachers are underestimating their own talent level."

"In what way?"

"Yesterday, I walked into the pre-K classroom, and the kids were reviewing the scientific method. I looked at them like I was confused, like, what the heck is going on in here? A room full of four-year-olds in white lab coats. Their teacher asked them, "What do all good experiments begin with?" And they all screamed, "QUESTIONS!""

Dahlia's eyes filled with tears. "They're *living it*. They get it. It's becoming ingrained in them—like, this is how we *think*. I don't know how many botched science experiments I saw in 10th grade. So just knowing what we're pushing teachers to do and knowing these ways of thinking and doing are being fostered makes me know these things will never be undone."

"We have a great team," Kristin replied. "We also seem to be working them too hard and not telling them enough about the great things they do—or even the things they need to do better."

"We still have a ways to go," said Dahlia. "I guess we just need to talk more as a group about the tension between where we ultimately want to be, and where we are right now."

◊   ◊   ◊   **B**   ◊   ◊   ◊

As Harvey's mom and dad settled in at the small table across from them, the Two Rebeccas resumed the pitch they'd perfected over the previous day and a half of parent/teacher conferences. "Thank you so much for coming," Ms. Schmidt began. "We have a lot of papers and information for you, to help you see more clearly how Harvey is doing, and where you can help."

"This is the level Harvey was reading at in September," Ms. Lebowitz added, pointing to the A–Z Fountas & Pinnell chart on the table between them. "And this is the level we want him to reach by the end of the year." She pulled out two different books and handed them to Harvey's parents. "Right now, this book reflects Harvey's current level. And *this* is the sort of book we expect him to be reading over the summer."

The first book was thin and filled with uncomplicated words and ideas; the second was thicker and more narrative-driven—a tangible symbol of a more engaged, motivated boy.

Harvey's mom shifted her youngest child from side to side, listening closely. "Did he show you his word list yesterday?" Ms. Lebowitz asked. "I tested him and he got every one right."

"I emptied out his book bag and saw it and he was like, 'Oh I forgot about that,'" she responded. "He's a work in progress, what can I say? But I know he likes you both, and he seems more positive about school than I've ever seen him before."

"We wanted to give you this notebook for Harvey to take with him on your upcoming trip to El Salvador," Ms. Lebowitz said. "While you're there over the holidays, encourage him to write about what he sees. The more we can get him in the habit of writing down his thoughts, the better off he'll be."

"I will," the mother replied. "He's never been to El Salvador before—he's never even been on a plane—so I'm sure he'll have a lot to say. Alright-y then," she said as she got up to make room for the next family. "Thank you, guys!"

Ms. Schmidt and Ms. Lebowitz looked down at the schedule to see which family was coming in next. Parent/teacher conferences were always a mad dash—two days of nearly constant appointments, 10 minutes at a time. In some of the meetings, they liked what they saw; in others, they felt like flies on the wall bearing witness to a family's particular brand of dysfunction. But either way, the conferences were an invaluable opportunity to learn more about their kids and their home lives—a way of seeing some of the factors that could only be guessed at during the school day.

After the final conference concluded, Rebecca Schmidt put on her running shoes and slipped out the back door of the school and straight into the dense canopy of Rock Creek Park. She was training for a marathon that spring—her first—and so most workdays ended this way, with a mind-clearing run. She loved the well-earned fatigue that followed her workouts, not to mention the deep sleep. She also yearned for the space to silently reflect on her work, and on her growing frustration with the inefficiencies of it all. There was only so much she could do in the current system, she'd reluctantly realized. And there was so much that needed to be done.

She passed other end-of-day runners on the path, each lost in private thoughts. Then she turned back toward home earlier than usual; everyone she knew was turning 30 that year, including herself, and that night was the latest in an endless string of birthday parties to attend.

Maybe it was just the symbolism of the number, or maybe it was more about the way the school year had started, but Ms. Schmidt had spent a lot of time that fall taking stock of her own life and deciding if it measured up to something she could feel good about. She thought about Harvey, who would be boarding his first plane in a few weeks. She thought about Lourdes, whose growing trust of her teachers had sparked real academic progress—and shown them just how vulnerable she was. And she thought about her friends' careers and weddings and birthday parties and pregnancies, and about Ms. Lebowitz's applications to grad school. Everyone would be moving on somewhere new in June; maybe it was time for her to move on, too.

Ms. Schmidt ran out of the park and past the back of the school, by the jungle gym and the soccer field and the faculty parking lot. On warmer days students lingered here to play until it got dark, but the weather had grown cold, and the playground was empty. Schmidt waved as Ms. Reid unlocked her car—the last one in the lot—and then turned up the leafy side street to complete the final two blocks of her run, to the group house she shared with four others, alongside the townhomes that had, not that long ago, been witness to the ravages of drug addiction or squatters or who knows what else, and were now seven-figure properties, adorned with welcoming Christmas decorations, reconstructed porches, and fresh coats of paint.

Ms. Schmidt followed the glow of the white lights to illuminate her path through the winter dark as she reached her front door. Her limbs felt heavy and tired, but she had 30 minutes to shower and get to the restaurant. It was time to see and be seen.

## CHAPTER FIVE

# Building a House

◊  ◊  ◊  **MV**  ◊  ◊  ◊

WHEN ROMEY PITTMAN was still a girl growing up on the Maryland farm her family had owned since 1725, she fantasized about becoming an outdoor child psychologist.

Most of her youth was spent outside—in the woods, with the cows, or visiting the tenant family that lived elsewhere on her farm's rolling acreage. So when she imagined herself working in a large office, with a dark wooden desk and a steady roster of parents who dropped their children off for therapy, eight-year-old Romey added an extra twist—a secret trap door just behind the desk, through which she and the children would escape to a beautiful woodland environment free from adult supervision. That's what would heal them, she decided. And their parents would never even need to know.

Years later, Romey had fashioned an adult life that honored the spirit of her childhood fantasy. As a college student, she designed her own major—she called it sociocultural development in education—and studied the ways different children from different cultures could expect very different experiences in school. And as a professional, she spent different stretches working with troubled boys and girls, chafing against the rigid structures of teaching at a traditional high school, and, eventually, founding her own.

Her efforts to build something lasting, however, always fell slightly short. What she'd learned was that the challenge of a really great education is almost all motivation. Yet every school she'd ever worked in, even the one she built herself, ended up stealing too much of their students' capacities for autonomy and meaning. Romey had designed her own school as a counterweight to the heavily structured environments in which she'd first taught, but what she realized was that the opposite extreme was just as problematic—in fact, all that happens if you replace pure structure with pure freedom is the same result: a purely mediocre place for learning. The art of building a great school came in striking the right balance between planning *and* improvisation—just like the art of building a great house.

The first house Romey built, the one that burned to the ground the night she and her husband moved in, took more than three years to complete. She was 22 and knew next to nothing about construction; the only thing she'd ever built was a homemade dulcimer. But she'd been sketching designs of houses her whole life, and she had a healthy dose of fearlessness, so she bought a 14-inch chainsaw, ignored everything she didn't know, and dove in.

Many months later, Romey stood before the most triumphant accomplishment of her life—a testament to the power of motivation, collaboration, and learning by doing. She'd cut down trees and peeled them by hand. She'd welcomed in friends from all corners who stayed for stretches and added their own personal touches. And on the night she and her husband threw a moving-in party to celebrate, Romey felt like she was sharing her personal masterpiece.

What she discovered, too late to help, was that she'd overlooked an essential piece of the puzzle: a single component of critical bracing in the chimney. No one was hurt, but the wood from the fire quickly spread to the wood from the cabin, and in a flash of light and heat all they'd worked for over the years—and everything Romey and her husband had acquired over the course of their lives—was gone.

She was devastated. And then, faster than she'd anticipated, she decided to start again. She used bales of straw this time for insulation, a lime plaster on the outside so the walls could breathe, and an earth plaster on the inside made of local clay, sand, and horse manure. It was fire-resistant and sustainable and completely unique. And this time, 11 months later, Romey and her husband moved in for good.

"With the second house, I really liked the balance we struck between a lot of forethought and planning, but also a lot of innovation in the moment," she explained one winter afternoon. "When you build something from scratch, you must have the right balance. The same is true for schools. Everything you do as a school designer is self-created based on need. That's where the expertise comes in—leaving enough room for the spontaneity to happen, and recognizing that you can't do everything on the fly."

As Zakiya Reid attached her computer to the LCD projector in Bancroft's library, members of her staff filed in and found seats at the eight rectangular tables in front of her. Each Wednesday morning they had school-wide faculty meetings, and on most days Zakiya was charged with sharing official slides from DCPS—a reflection of the central office's effort to impose a level of quality control across a vast and diverse network of neighborhood schools.

On this day, the slides were about the district's new report card. Like most of the district's newest programs or procedures, the report card reflected an effort to make DCPS more standards-based. Zakiya had reviewed the slides the night before. She liked that teachers were being asked to choose one of four numbers to chart overall progress in each category (1 = doesn't meet the standard; 2 = approaches; 3 = meets; 4 = exceeds), and one of four letters to chart progress toward each specific skill (S = secure; D = developing; B = beginning; N = not introduced). She also liked that although the categories for the tested subjects—English and math—had the longest lists of skills to assess, DCPS had created separate lists for some of the categories that had, amidst the current test obsession, fallen to the wayside: science, social studies, music, art, health—even personal & social skills.

What Ms. Reid didn't like was that she was about to introduce a standards-based report card to a room of educators that didn't do standards-based grading. Once again, her teachers were being asked to do something before they'd been equipped to do it well (or at all). And that sort of misalignment could only mean one thing—if the connections weren't clear to teachers, they definitely wouldn't be clear to parents, students, or anyone else.

"Good morning, everyone," she began as a few final teachers filed in. "As you know, DCPS just instituted new report card guidelines.

What we're trying to do is standardize across the school—and the city—so parents can get feedback on their child that's as accurate as possible. If we're going to do that, though, we can't all be giving kids 4s just because we feel like it—we're going to have to start *really* talking about where kids are at, and how we know."

Ms. Lebowitz shifted in her seat and crossed her arms. She didn't disagree with anything her principal was saying—in fact, she supported all of it. But she'd also come to believe that the changes Ms. Reid sought at Bancroft were still frustratingly far away. There simply wasn't enough support at the school for this sort of shift, as evidenced by the conversation that emerged when Ms. Reid switched to a slide illustrating the way Bancroft was nested within the larger network of DCPS.

Prior to Reid's arrival—which coincided with Rhee's—Bancroft's former principal presided over an era when local schools were much freer to determine their own individual course of action. District mandates still came down from time to time—but schools typically decided whether the mandate was a good fit. If it was, they complied. And if it wasn't, they kept doing what they were already doing.

That legacy of minimal oversight spawned its own set of unofficial norms and values, one of which had proven particularly resonant: "You have to be subversive to be successful." Another might as well have been the educational version of the well-worn revolutionary battle cry: "Don't tread on me." And so, when principals like Ms. Reid came in with district-issued PowerPoint presentations with pictures of a pressure cooker, some saw it as their responsibility to resist.

"As you can see, we're part of a formal network now," Reid explained. "It's no longer possible to just keep doing what we were doing and not expect folks in the district office to notice. I know that means sometimes some of you feel like you're in a pressure cooker. I do, too, and that can feel uncomfortable and time-sensitive."

"I don't want to be cooked!" yelled a teacher from the back of the room. Some teachers applauded. Ms. Lebowitz rolled her eyes. Ms. Reid swallowed and continued.

"I know no one wants to be cooked. I also know no one wants to see D.C. continue as a failing system. That means we have to take seriously what the numbers tell us—and the painful truth is that too many of our kids still can't read. We may want to see ourselves as being separate from the reality that we're one of the country's lowest performing districts, but we can't be separate from that. We *are* part of that."

Later, as the meeting ended and everyone left the library to return to their rooms, Ms. Reid studied the body language of her teachers. She knew a lot of them were likely on their way out—including the Two Rebeccas, who, despite Ms. Reid's efforts, simply didn't have enough support systems in place to keep them there. The fault lines were becoming too clearly drawn.

Ms. Reid had felt that mixture of certainty and helplessness before. She knew quitting her job at the IRS was the right thing to do—and she remembered sitting in her car the day she walked out and crying out of fear for her unknown future. She was certain that leaving the freedom of the charter world for the structure of the district was the right decision—and she was still struggling to adjust to its particular inefficiencies. And she knew she needed to call her grandmother the night before her second triple bypass surgery, because she was certain it was going to be the last time they spoke.

Her grandmother knew it, too. "I thought you were going to wait around and be the woman on the Smucker's jar on the *Today* show— celebrating your 100th birthday!" Zakiya had joked. "I don't know if that's going to happen," her grandmother replied. "You told me not to eat all those ribs, and I told you what I'm telling you again now—I'm not going to deprive myself. We all have only one life to live."

The morning of the last day of the first semester, Berenice Pernalete woke up and listened to see if any of her three roommates were already using the bathroom. Usually she was the first person up—and usually at 5:00 A.M. The house was old, and the bathroom was dirty, so she slipped on her flip-flops, grabbed her bag of toiletries, and then hopped into a shower with a floor so slanted she had to anchor herself to avoid tipping over.

The house was also cold and drafty, especially by late December, and one of her roommates had a cat that would attack her ankles as she passed. But Berenice didn't mind; optimistic by nature, she'd slip on her Mundo Verde T-shirt, khakis, and tennis shoes, grab her book bag, walk out the door, and call her mom for some *Jarabe de lengua*, grateful for the daily challenge of doing something meaningful and important.

Lately, their conversations had been all about the changes Berenice was starting to see in her students, and their growing level of comfort with Spanish. She was particularly excited that morning—it was parent/teacher conference day, which meant she got to personally deliver the good news to her students' families and celebrate their good work together. Berenice got off the train and felt the familiar rush of air as she came up the escalators to street level. I'm young, she thought to herself. I'm doing important work. And I'm in the right place.

Berenice entered her room and began to clean it up—the previous day's aftercare always left it in disarray. Fifteen minutes later, it was ready for visitors—clean, orderly, welcoming, and blanketed with careful and colorful examples of student work.

Berenice had two goals for her meetings: to show parents the work their children produced as a result of the school's first-ever learning expedition, on water; and to help them understand how she taught them Spanish. She organized the children's drawings to correspond with the order in which their families would arrive, and placed Jimmy's on top.

The cadence of a parent/teacher conference is always a tenuous one. On one side, the teacher is eager to share information and observations, some of which may be uncomfortable for the parent to hear; on the other side, the parent is eager to provide explanations, some of which may stem from the deepest layers of anxiety and self-consciousness. Berenice knew that sort of dynamic could be at play when Jimmy's mother arrived for her conference. She also knew a bad report would only make things more difficult for him at home. She thought carefully about what to share, and how to describe what she saw in ways his mother would be most likely to hear.

Jimmy was the student Berenice worried about the most. Sweet and needy, he arrived most mornings asking for hugs, perhaps the result of his dad no longer being in the picture. On several days, Berenice noticed he was covered with scratches; sometimes he wore makeup to cover his bruises. She called Child Protective Services to tell them what she'd observed, but nothing changed—just a steady rotation of the long list of family members dropping him off and picking him up, none of whom seemed well-tuned to Jimmy's neediness, or his vulnerability. On more than one occasion Berenice watched as they would leave the building to head home, Jimmy slowly falling blocks behind the pace of his caretakers, one wrong turn away from being lost in the city.

Jimmy's desperation had made it difficult for him to make friends. The other children could tell something was different about him, and so even if they weren't mean, they also weren't lining up to jeopardize their own reputations just to make him feel better.

Berenice saw all of this, and did what she could to make her classroom as safe as possible for students like Jimmy. She worked with the children to establish a set of class norms—behavioral standards that specified how everyone wanted to be treated by one another. She acted swiftly and fairly when she saw children misbehaving. She was never cruel. And she did what she could to accept the painful truth that she could only do so much; the biggest influence on her children's behavior, good or bad, came from their families. What she did was gather up daily acts of kindness, curiosity, or insight, like raindrops. And, when it was necessary, she helped the children pour out their feelings of sadness or rage, like floodwaters.

As Jimmy entered the classroom with his mother and baby sister, Berenice smiled widely and raised her eyebrows. "¡*Jimmy! Cómo estás?*" He leaned in for a hug.

"*Estoy bien*, Ms. Berenice. This is my mother."

"I've been so excited for this meeting," Berenice continued in Spanish, "because Jimmy has done some great work this semester. Here, let me show you."

Across the hall, just past the station of fresh coffee and oranges, Molly Howard took a sip of water from her Nalgene bottle, reviewed her schedule of meetings, and thought about what she wanted to highlight about each student. Parents came into conferences to feel good about their child's school, and there were plenty of things to feel good about—it's just that Molly wasn't sure if the water expedition was one of them.

It had been a mixed bag: cool in some ways, a missed opportunity in others. Berenice and Molly had never done anything like it before, and although the kids loved visiting the local hotel and designing their own personal doorknockers—which the hotel agreed to place on guests' doors to promote water conservation—Molly wasn't sure anyone had actually learned anything lasting. Maybe five-year-olds were still too young to explore a complicated issue like where water came from, where it went, and why we should pay attention to both. And how was a project that spanned so many weeks, and took up so much class time and energy, helping her students learn how to read, particularly the ones still struggling to master the basics?

Molly knew what it felt like to struggle. As a child, it had taken her a long time to learn to read—much longer than most of her classmates—and she'd always wondered what it would have been like if she'd had someone more supportive by her side. Instead, she remembers being made to feel stupid, spending second grade in a remedial program, and stumbling through her early years in a fog of frustration. Then something clicked, and by third grade she found herself out of remedial education, and in the gifted & talented program. By the time she graduated from high school, she'd completed 16 AP classes and gained admission to the Ivy League.

What drove Molly was the idea that she could help fix some of her students the way she had gradually fixed herself. And yet as the first semester neared its end, she still felt overwhelmed by the challenges they faced—particularly the boys.

Elan was one that kept her up at night. A sturdy boy with large, round brown eyes and cocoa skin, Elan spent most days facing in the opposite direction of the rest of the class. When Molly first tested him at the beginning of the year, he could only recognize six letters. Often, he would run around the room biting and spitting. The day before parent/teacher conferences, he'd circled the carpet pounding everyone's toes. Whenever Molly made a move toward him, he would sprint around the room, eat people's lunches, or run out of the classroom—anything but what he was being asked to do.

Finally out of options, she'd escorted him to the office, where Dahlia was waiting.

"Do you know why Ms. Molly brought you here?" Dahlia asked, kneeling down to reach Elan's eye-level.

"Because I was trying to be mean to people?" he said, his gaze fixed on the wall behind her.

"Why are you doing that?"

"I don't know."

Dahlia called Elan's father, and handed him the phone. Elan listened quietly for several minutes, and then handed it back to her.

"What did your father say to you?" Dahlia asked.

"He said I shouldn't be mean to people. You don't know what he said because he said it in the African voice." Elan smiled.

"Yeah, Amharic," Dahlia replied.

"Oh, you know that voice!" Elan's eyes widened as he looked directly at her.

He's negotiating the world through three different languages, Molly thought. He's getting dropped off at 7:15 and picked up at 6:30. His parents are getting divorced. And he can't even focus long enough for us to take an accurate temperature of what he knows and doesn't know. This boy is *so angry*. And I have no idea how to reach him.

Molly greeted Elan's mother as she entered the room. Elan sat in his chair for a second before bounding off to Molly's makeshift library. There weren't many things at school that held Elan's attention, but picture books were one.

"I think Elan's on the verge of some breakthrough progress," Molly told his mother. "We just have to stick with it. When children are learning to read, sometimes it can feel like we're having them read the same thing a thousand times and asking them to point at the words. But then something clicks, and they realize the code, and they see that these four shapes make a word. It hasn't happened for Elan yet, but what I've seen in some of the other children is that that moment triggers a wild curiosity.

"Every day I ask the kids, 'Where are we going today?'" Elan looked up from his book as he heard the familiar words of his teacher. "My hope is that your son will start asking that question more as he learns to read. The appeal lies in the mystery."

◊ ◊ ◊ **MV** ◊ ◊ ◊

"In Spanish, we learn to read with syllables," Berenice explained for the thirteenth consecutive time. "The first thing you learn are the vowel sounds, which never change. Then you start adding simple consonants, then complex consonants, and then grouping. It never changes. And I think kids love that part because it's so consistent."

Growing up, Berenice had learned Spanish the way everyone else did—from syllable books known as *silabarios*. Unlike the way most children learn English, the text in those books had no meaning; it was strictly a decoding instrument, which meant it couldn't really help with comprehension.

Berenice was in search of a better way. "I strongly believe that's the reason why it's so hard to be a writer in Latin America," she explained to one parent. "The authors that we celebrate the most are the authors that have been dead for 20 years. And I don't see a huge wealth of new books being written—our kids are not being taught to think critically. They lose interest in reading. So I'm trying to build a different approach.

"The key is our emphasis on whole to part, not part to whole. It digs deeply into comprehension, and on learning a text, talking about it, even if you don't understand everything. I think a really good way to make a solid curriculum is to combine good simple consonants with sight words that are not easily decodable but are easily recognizable as a picture. Combining words that are simple—'My mom has a mop'—you can create a story but you have to be really creative. And that's what your daughter is doing every day at Mundo Verde."

◊ ◊ ◊ **MV** ◊ ◊ ◊

As the first semester neared its conclusion, Kristin Scotchmer felt grateful for the emerging sense of familiarity to her brand new life. The chaos of dropoff and pickup at the school had begun to subside. The rhythms of the faculty had started to settle. The give and take between them had reaffirmed Kristin's choice to make Dahlia Mundo Verde's first principal. And as she prepared her presentation for the last board meeting of the calendar year, she felt proud of all the good news she was about to share.

Kristin unpacked the bottle of wine and the crackers from her grocery bag, waiting for the board members to arrive. By 8:30 P.M., all nine members were huddled around the conference table, their amalgam of laptops making a small space feel even more confined.

"I'm particularly excited for this meeting," Kristin began, "and not just because we're about to complete our first semester as a school. As you know, part of the challenge of my job is to keep looking ahead, and I think I've found our future home. Let me tell you about it."

The day before, Kristin had parked her car at the corner of 1st and P Streets NW. Not that long ago, it was a part of the city she would have known almost nothing about. Now, as she stepped out to visit the potential future home for her school, she was imagining what it would take to move in.

To her right, Kristin heard the sounds of children at play. She walked over to get a closer look and saw two signs in front of the square, sturdy school that dominated the block. One proclaimed the school's current occupant, the Dorothy Height Community Academy Public Charter School. The other, still etched in stone over the school's front doors, gave its original name: Armstrong Manual Training School. First built in 1901, it had been designed to teach practical, manual skills in honor of the philosophy of Booker T. Washington. Kristin watched as a stern-faced African American woman provided careful watch over the carefree movements of the children. Behind them, the sky was cluttered with cranes towering over a sea of new construction projects.

Kristin crossed the street in search of the school she had come to inspect. She walked past the Faith & Hope Full Gospel Holiness Church, where a homeless man was curled up in the fetal position outside the front door. She walked a few steps farther and the din of jackhammers and children's voices disappeared. It became completely silent; she was the only person on the street.

Kristin looked one way, past the canopy of trees, and saw a faded, rust-stained sign: SLATER SCHOOL. Many of its windows were broken, and much of the red brick exterior had begun to crumble. She walked farther and found a fully restored playground, just past a 10-foot-tall chain link fence. All of its slides and jungle gyms were freshly painted, and the wall just beyond it had been dressed up with a colorful mural of a carousel. But there were no children here to give it life.

Kristin walked farther to inspect the second abandoned school on the block, which abutted the other side of the playground. First built in 1891, the Langston School had become a homeless shelter in 1997, but for the past several years it had been completely vacant. The building was too unstable to allow prospective tenants to enter it, so Kristin studied it from the outside. She could see why they weren't allowed in—it was extremely run-down—but its original charm was still apparent, including the large stone-carved Star of David at its center.

Still alone, Kristin searched for the city official who would usher her into the one school she *would* tour, directly across the street from these two. Formerly known as J. F. Cook, it had been among the 23 DCPS schools closed in 2008 for low enrollment under then-chancellor Michelle Rhee. In its final year of operations, 13% of Cook's students were proficient in reading and 14% in math.

Like Slater and Langston, Cook was originally built as a sort of two-block campus to serve nearby post-Civil War African American settlements. Kristin peered through a chain link fence to admire its large red front doors; separate entrances framed either side, one for BOYS, one for GIRLS. Her guide arrived and they walked around the back to enter.

Inside, it was evident how much damage had been done in just three years; all the sinks in the building had been stolen, along with all the copper piping. Condoms littered the floor, and pools of water confirmed the shoddy state of the roof. But as she walked the wide hallways, Kristin fell in love with the ways it felt like a school. By the time she entered its open auditorium and sat in one of its old wooden seats, Kristin was doing the inner calculations of how it could be rebuilt: That concrete exterior could become a vegetable garden and the green space for our outdoor classroom. That second floor could handle all of our plans for expansion. The walk from the New York Avenue Metro station is only four blocks. And the move would position us to become a positive part of the changes taking place in the neighborhood.

"With your permission," Kristin explained to her board members, "I would like to begin working on a proposal to put in an offer on the Cook school. The city is asking us to project out for 10 years, and to submit our proposal to the department that deals with surplus buildings. I don't know who else is interested, but I've been told that the D.C. Council will 'dispose' the property to whomever wins out."

"We've had an amazing start to the year," Kristin continued, "but we all know we need a new space if we want to keep building toward our dream. And I think this is the place where we can do so."

◊   ◊   ◊   MV   ◊   ◊   ◊

After the final families had picked up the last remaining children in aftercare, Dahlia Aguilar gathered all of her teachers in the conference room for a final check-in before the beginning of winter break. "Teaching is one of the most complex activities you could possibly engage in," she began. "You make more than 71,000 decisions every day. That's why it's so difficult to evaluate what we do, but I think if you had to boil it down, it might be these things."

Dahlia directed everyone's attention to the pieces of butcher paper she'd hung on the walls around the room. Each one had a different title: Engaging students in learning. Planning instruction. Creating an effective environment. Developing as a professional. Assessing student learning and growth. Organizing subject matter.

"Before we all scatter for some well-deserved vacation time, take a few minutes to think about each indicator, and write down what you think it will look like when we're doing it well." Dahlia handed everyone a magic marker, eager to see what her young staff would select out of their own practices to promote. The group was slow to engage, however, and few descriptions were added. Most of the teachers stood around awkwardly; perhaps in their minds, Dahlia wondered, vacation has already begun.

"Let's try this another way," she interrupted. "Break into pairs and work together to try and find five indicators of each competency." As the teachers paired off, Dahlia checked in with Romey, wondering what accounted for the relative silence. "Everyone's looking a little freaked out," Romey replied. "It may be that this feels like one thing too many."

When the whole group reconvened, the pieces of butcher paper had longer lists of indicators, but the faces of the teachers still seemed troubled. "Any noticings, wows, or wonders up there?" Dahlia asked.

"I notice that very little of what people described is what we actually learned to do in graduate school," Berenice replied.

"I wonder if five-year-olds are capable of reflecting fully on what they've learned," Molly added.

"And I really wonder if they can do it in Spanish," said another teacher.

"Perhaps," Dahlia said, "but I don't want you to worry about any of those things for now. This has been an amazing start to what we all hope will become an amazing school. I'm so proud of all of you. Have a wonderful and well-deserved break, and we'll revisit some of these things in January."

Later that night, back at her apartment, Dahlia debated whether she should venture out to the poetry slam a friend had encouraged her to attend.

After the end of her marriage, Dahlia had left behind most of her belongings—including her writing. She didn't like returning to her former house if she could avoid it. But a friend who knew of Dahlia's talent and of her recent return to putting pen on paper, had pushed her to join him and make her work more public.

At first, Dahlia wished she had thought to pack up her old poems and take them with her. Then she read through some of her more recent work, still debating whether to go, and she realized she had some pieces worth sharing.

After her father died on September 16, 1996—the anniversary of Mexico's independence from Spain—Dahlia had nightly dreams about him. Those dreams had returned recently, sparking her motivation to resume writing. While her son played at her feet, Dahlia read through a recent draft, imagining what it would feel like to recite the words into a microphone and await a live audience's reaction:

*Wrench, you say*

*I know this is a trick,*
*Your latest trampa, at best an illusion*
*(sometimes you ask for a towel or a beer, just like you used to)*
*you have returned*
*a fox visiting, but swift*

*wrench, you repeat*

*we always loved sweat in July*
*though we complained*
*you stop droplets before the salt flows into your eyes*
*with the back of your hand*
*the calluses on your hands grow impatient*

*wrench, mi'ja*

*your frustration surfaces*
*same as your disappointment*
*when I didn't know*
*regular from Phillips*
*wrench from pliers*
*or the right-size nail*
    *does that look like an inch*

*Maybe lingers in me*
*Perhaps resides like hope*
*It turns me and I trust it*
*So I reach for it*

*The wrench*

*Day turns to night*
*Hope hollows*
*And*
*I wake*

She put the paper down and looked at her son. There was no one else to look after him. I'll go next time. After too many years of losing touch with the things that made her happiest—writing, dancing, and doing whatever she could to proactively feel *alive*—everything in her life felt new again. Each day was placing her on the edge of success or failure. And it was all going to work itself out.

# PART II

# SPRING

## CHAPTER SIX

# Our School

◊ ◊ ◊ **MV** ◊ ◊ ◊

ON AN UNSEASONABLY warm morning in early January, Yolanda Hood entered the Washington Convention Center. It was busy inside, especially for a Saturday. On the main floor, she passed packs of aspiring entrepreneurs, dressed to impress at the Millionaire Success Network. She walked to the edge of a landing and looked down at the lower level; green strobe lights twisted and turned in sync with the rhythmic thumping of the cheerleading competition, where thin girls in bright ribbons and matching eyeliner were competing in the most important event of their young lives.

Yolanda stepped onto the escalator and headed upstairs, reviewing her questions and her notes. This was not her first Charter Schools Expo, but it was the last one she would get to attend before she and her husband finally had to choose a school for their son, Hunter.

Although Hunter was not yet three—the year most D.C. children started school, thanks to a 2008 law that set the goal of providing pre-K to every three- and four-year old in the district by 2014—his mother had been researching options for two years. When she first started calling to ask about open houses, the secretaries she spoke to thought she was crazy. "Why are you doing this now?" they would cluck at her. "Come back when he's actually old enough to go to school." But Yolanda Hood didn't like to wait. "Plan for the worst but hope for the best," she often said. "*And* worry, but know that worrying is as effective as trying to solve an algebra equation by chewing bubble gum. The real troubles in your life are apt to be the things that never crossed your worried mind, the kind that blindside you at 4:00 P.M. on some idle Tuesday."

She reached the third floor, ran her hands across thick braids, and stepped off the escalator in heavy work boots, her large keychain jingling loudly as she did. It was still a few minutes before the Expo officially began, and scores of parents were already lined up along a wall outside the main ballroom. Volunteers in light green CHOOSE YOUR SCHOOL T-shirts sat behind registration tables, handing out thick books profiling every public school in D.C. and tote bags that read: *I am public charter schools and I vote.*

The doors to the ballroom opened. Yolanda avoided the army of strollers to assess the scene—and maximize her time. Half the room was filled with vendors who were here to pitch the charter operators themselves: purveyors of business furniture, or construction, or catering services. Yolanda brushed past them and began her line of questioning at the first school table she saw: Mundo Verde Bilingual Public Charter School.

A tall, slender woman wearing fur-lined boots, skinny jeans and a Mundo Verde T-shirt greeted Yolanda as she walked up. "Good morning! I'm Molly Howard and I teach kindergarten. What would you like to know about our school?"

While her teachers and parent volunteers fielded questions from each new wave of prospective families, Kristin Scotchmer helped the most excited among them complete their application—in reality, little more than a name and address—on the spot. The room was crowded and close, and it was becoming hard to hear over the din of so many simultaneous conversations, a situation made worse by the periodic announcements over the loudspeaker: "Get your tickets ready!" a female voice barked. "I'm about to draw the first raffle. Also, kids yoga will begin in five minutes!"

Kristin looked around at the other tables. You could learn a lot about a school by seeing how they chose to present themselves. Mundo Verde's table was framed by large photos of students. Another school's table displayed printouts of its performance on the high-stakes test for the city, the DC-CAS. And one high school, well known for its athletic prowess, sent the entire cheerleading squad and several members of its championship football team.

Kristin got up from the table to listen in on a conversation between one of her parents and a prospective mother named Karen. "We had to do a complete leap of faith," the parent explained. "We were on vacation and our daughter had already enrolled somewhere else. But then we got the call from Mundo Verde in mid-September, and we decided that even though she'd begun the year at another school, this school was worth the risk. We're so happy we did."

"I just feel the whole process is so insanely disorganized," Karen responded, unconvinced. "Every school says they do all these amazing things—no offense—but how can you really know? And some of the newest schools like yours don't even have *buildings* yet! How can I invest my time if I don't even know where the school is going to be located?"

Karen moved on to another table. I followed to hear more about her experiences and what she was looking for. "I don't have an education background," she said, "so I don't know what characterizes a sign of success. I was at one open house and their first-graders were working on their letters. Is that appropriate? My daughter is three and she's known her letters for a while now.

"I'm absolutely not thinking about our neighborhood school," she continued, her large brown eyes wide with intensity. "But I'm also biased towards public schools and schools you can walk to. I won't compromise—but I also don't know what that means. And meanwhile I just heard that one of the older charter schools isn't even taking applications for preschool because every available spot was taken up by siblings. How is this choice?"

For parents like Karen Copeland, the notion of school choice was a complicated one to embrace. "I worry that what we're doing is fragmenting the city," she confessed. "The degree of independence is breaking us all up—it would be different if there were equal numbers of high-quality DCPS schools, but there aren't. And the logistics are so brutal. You've got the public schools, and you have to commit to them by the end of February. But then the charters don't hold their lotteries until April. Why do we tolerate a system where there is constant movement until September or October? It's things like that that make me so tense. I can't even get beyond the cursory 'We love it' or 'We're a Montessori school' or 'We're a language-immersion school.' I keep waiting to hear something that will unlock the code for finding the best place for my daughter."

Growing up in upstate New York, Karen benefited from the most familiar of American educational codes: the security (and predictability) of her neighborhood school. "I went to public school my whole life," she said. "I graduated with kids I'd been with since sixth grade. That's why when we moved to D.C., I picked my neighborhood because it felt like a real *neighborhood*. And it's been what I'd hoped for—I know and like my neighbors—but the nearest school is no good, people are already moving away, and either way none of our kids will attend the same schools."

As her daughter, Lia, neared school age, Karen and her husband faced a dilemma: stay where they were and subject themselves to the whims of the school lotteries, or move out of the city altogether. And although Karen was intrigued enough to spend a Saturday afternoon in a convention center, she still wasn't sure if it would be worth it in the end. "Why am I spending all this time visiting charters when I could end up 500th on every list? I think I might as well apply to all of them and then do the research when or if I get in, since there aren't any penalties for holding a spot if you get one. But I realize that also makes me part of the problem.

"Ultimately, my biggest issue with the charters is that most of them don't have a building they can count on. You cannot build a sense of community if you think it's going to get pulled out from under you year after year. Period."

Yolanda Hood felt less ambivalent. A D.C. native who met her husband in high school, she planned to apply to every charter school with a preschool program. "I like the choices," she explained. "The whole neighborhood school was a good idea, but not now—a lot of folks move into neighborhoods they know nothing about. And anyway, just because you live in a certain area doesn't mean your school options should suck."

Two years ago, Yolanda's search had begun in the neighborhood schools she attended growing up. But not anymore. "The traditional public schools still assume, 'You'll come. We'll be here.' They don't realize that now is the time people are saying education is free and I'm going to get the best one I can get."

Four hours later, the cheerleading competition had awarded its trophies, the Millionaire Success Network had wrapped up its seminars, and the Charter School Expo vendors had packed up their promotional displays. A few schools and parents remained, including Kristin Scotchmer. Of everything she'd done since deciding to take the plunge and start a school, this was the first time she'd done something for the second time. And it felt different this time around, now that the idea of her school was not just an idea but a real place with real teachers and families and kids. One thing, however, felt the same—the bittersweet feeling of having all these conversations and meeting all these interesting people, and knowing that some of them would become a part of the Mundo Verde family, and most of them would not.

Yolanda Hood was also still there, asking one last question at the last school table she would reach before the Expo officially closed. She'd made it through just two of the 10 rows of schools—one table at a time. But it was a good start, she thought, and it was about to be open house season. By the time the deadlines rolled around, she'd be ready to make her choice.

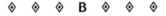

◊  ◊  ◊  **B**  ◊  ◊  ◊

On the morning of her first day back after winter break, Rebecca Lebowitz walked through Malcolm X Park, clutching her thermos of green tea and feeling a sense of dread.

She had been up late the night before, reading *The Girl with the Dragon Tattoo* and exchanging texts with Schmidt in which each confessed her reluctance to return. "Teacher-controllable factors" was a motto Michelle Rhee had used often—and that had come to define Lebowitz's personal philosophy about her work. Her job was to control

100% of what happens in her classroom, and if a child comes to school, no matter what situation they're in and no matter how severe their deficiencies, they're in her care. That philosophy hadn't changed, but she couldn't help but feel that DCPS was, in her words, "a hot mess," and that an already-difficult job was being made unsustainable because of all the inefficiencies that surrounded her.

In her opinion, people were still reeling from Rhee's departure; special education was glaringly insufficient; essential positions were being cut with each new budget; the disparities among schools were great and growing; it was still too hard to fire people; and accountability measures were not as good as they should be. She also felt the transience of the city in which she lived. All of her friends, it seemed, were moving on—and Rebecca Lebowitz didn't like feeling left behind.

She walked past the Josephine Butler Parks Center, on the corner of the park and 15th Street. The winter had been mild, so there was no snow on the ground, just brown grass that contrasted against the bright yellow exterior of the Parks Center. In a mailbox right around the corner from here, a week earlier, she had dropped in her two graduate school applications—one to Harvard, the other to Columbia. She imagined the stark differences of either possibility: the cities, the schools, the existing networks of friends and family. In the past, she had wanted things so badly she lost sight of whether she actually wanted the thing or just got swept up in wanting to *want* something. But that didn't feel like the case here.

Rebecca had always known she would be, like the rest of her family, an education lifer. But she also knew that, at 24, she "needed more personal data" about herself. She needed to explore other things, figure out her own goals, figure out her next steps personally and socially, and understand more deeply what she really wanted. And as she neared the school and the feeling of dread returned to her gut, she knew that sort of growth couldn't happen at Bancroft, not yet at least.

As Lebowitz walked into her room, Rebecca Schmidt was already there waiting for her, a look of distress on her face, surrounded by a hallway full of furniture. The floors of the school had been waxed over the holiday, and no one had bothered to return the desks and chairs to their rightful places. The day's final round of lesson planning would have to wait.

Lebowitz saw it as a symbolic start. The metal legs of the desks scraped across the newly waxed floors as they worked quickly. "Why do they do this to us?" she asked rhetorically. "It's like a slap in the face."

While the two teachers hurriedly reassembled their room, Bancroft's students gathered downstairs in the gymnasium, waiting to be dismissed. The gym was directly across from the school's three front doors, so it was drafty inside. Parents hugged teachers and gave their children final instructions; for some, the time off was making for a difficult re-entry. One older mother near the door leaned down to give her son, buried beneath his oversized brown hoodie and blue camouflage backpack, some final encouragement. She held his hand and stroked it gently while new arrivals shuffled past them, each figure a miniature arctic explorer, watery eyes peering out between the narrow slit separating hat and scarf. Finally the mother readied to leave and the son joined with a trio of boys sitting cross-legged and swapping stories. She lingered at the door as he looked back once, and then not again.

By the time the students arrived, room 121 looked as it had when they'd last inhabited it, two weeks earlier. The children came in, hung up their backpacks and coats, and gradually made their way to the edge of the carpet, where Ms. Schmidt had them go around in a circle and share something fun they did over the break. These daily shares were an essential part of building a classroom culture of support and encouragement, and it was especially important on the first day back from a winter break that was, depending on your home life, somewhere between wonderful and horrible. "If someone says something that you also did, step into the middle with them and say, 'Me too!'" Ms. Schmidt explained cheerily. Some students responded in kind; others opted out, and a few, like Rodger, didn't seem to even understand the words people were speaking.

Ms. Lebowitz sat in a circle at the head of the rug, staring straight ahead. The second semester was only minutes old, and she was already tired.

◊   ◊   ◊   **MV**   ◊   ◊   ◊

Across town, on the second floor of the office building their teachers had transformed months earlier into a school, the Lions and Zebras returned to new seat assignments and a wall full of their own beautiful drawings, framed by black construction paper and below a colorful new ART sign. Their landscape portraits were from the first semester exhibition on water, and alongside the drawings were the children's short poems on the same subject:

*I love you H20,*
*You save the fish and*
*The sea.*
*You save the whole earth.*

The Zebras gathered in their morning circle. Albert was bursting with happiness to be back. As the rug filled up, he put his arms around the children on either side of him, smiling widely. Freya recoiled at the touch, but Albert was unfazed. He was right where he wanted to be.

Stephen was among the late arrivals. He hung up his coat underneath the list of each student's hopes and dreams for the year—his own was "to do the monkey bars and be good"—still resembling a child caught between worlds. Whereas many of his classmates came from nearby neighborhoods, Stephen lived a full three bus routes away. Tall and thick for his age, Stephen lived in a neighborhood that required a certain amount of toughness to survive. Once, an older boy stole his bike while he was still riding it. Yet here he was again, after two weeks away, sitting in a circle and singing songs—or, more accurately, opting *not* to sing them.

Still, Stephen defied easy characterizations. More than other children, he burned with emotional intelligence and a desire for acceptance. That intelligence popped out whenever there was something to engage his imagination, as there was when Molly asked the class what they wanted to learn most before the school year was over. "I want to learn what 1,000 + 1,000 is," he volunteered with wonder, the façade of toughness falling away and reminding you that he was just five years old.

Just as quickly, however, Stephen's toggle switch between toughness and vulnerability would flip, as it did later that morning when he and Bruno got into a shoving match. The children were working at math stations, tracing their hands and legs when the shoving started. Molly rushed across the room to separate the boys. Bruno seemed merely inconvenienced at being caught; but Stephen was instantly agitated and in tears.

"He pushed me first!" Stephen yelled.

"I didn't say you didn't and I didn't say you did," Molly calmly replied. "Calm down and sit with me on the carpet so we can talk this through."

The three crouched down while the class work around them continued, and Molly asked each boy to explain what happened. "Stephen took my paper and I tried to get it back and he pushed me," said Bruno. Stephen jumped up on his feet to counter the allegation, tears streaming down his face.

"Stephen, you'll get your turn, I promise. Now why did he push you, Bruno? I just want to make sure I get this right."

Molly listened to Bruno recount the events, while her co-teacher Jen kept an eye on everyone else. "Now it's your turn, Stephen. What was going on in the class? Oh, you were tracing your foot! That's great. So why did you take his paper? I'm just trying to understand what was happening."

Then Stephen gave his side of things. No longer crying, he twirled his thumbs rapidly as he spoke. "OK," Molly continued, "now it's time for all of us to talk and re-create what happened. It sounds like we both made mistakes. What were they?"

"I took his paper," Stephen said.

"I punched Stephen," Bruno confessed.

"Stephen, I think you made one more mistake," said his teacher. "Do you know what it was?"

"I pushed him," Stephen added.

"That's right," said Molly. "And both of you broke the rule of being a good friend. How can we make it better?"

While Bruno remained silent, Stephen said what was in his heart. "We could start being real friends and hanging out because that's all I really want to do."

"Alright. You guys are missing the math activity. I think it makes sense for you to be partners in that activity. But first it's time to apologize. Bruno, do you want a hug, a handshake, or a high-five?"

Bruno opted for the handshake; Stephen followed suit. And 10 minutes after the fight, the two boys were back at work and tracing each other's feet. Molly moved on to check in with a group of students working at a table, allowing herself a brief moment to celebrate this small success, and reflect on how far she'd come since the start of the year.

◊   ◊   ◊   **MV**   ◊   ◊   ◊

As nice as those small successes felt, Molly Howard still wasn't sure if Mundo Verde was the place for her. "I realized this fall that I was pretty unhappy," she told me just before the first staff meeting of the new semester. "I was unhappy with a lot of things. And I knew I wouldn't be coming back without saying something—and that the changes required were small.

"My stress wasn't from the kids," she continued. "It was from other dynamics. It was from having to do everything for the first time and know that the school was doing it for the first time as well. It was from wondering how to do an expedition and link it to standards, and feel like I was basically on my own to figure it out. And it was from feeling like I wasn't getting the feedback I needed to really get better at this job. Because this job is really, really *hard*. There needs to be more of a spirit that we're all in this together. And we're not there yet. I get rewards every day—but getting rewards from five-year-olds feels different from getting them from your peers."

To get ready for the new semester, Molly and the rest of the staff had spent a Saturday at Romey Pittman's farm, outlining personal and professional goals for the second semester. Molly's were simple: professionally, to get better at differentiating instruction; and personally, to get better at asking for what she needed. "I love the idea of our school," she added as she opened the door to the conference room. "But I won't put myself through another year like this."

Inside, Dahlia Aguilar was waiting for her teachers to arrive, both excited and nervous about the meeting they were about to have. She'd heard—from Molly and others—that it was important for people to feel more involved in the decisions that affected the school. She supported the idea in theory. She also knew that in reality she and Kristin had to make decisions—lots of them—rapidly and on the go, based on quick back and forth conversations in their office and partial information. There were so many fires to put out—from finding a building to recruiting new staff members to developing an assessment system— and the timetable of those decisions didn't always lend itself to a deliberative process. Besides, Dahlia Aguilar's professional models had not been those sorts of principals. No one had held her hand.

She remembered the day when she was 14 and her father had been teaching her to bodysurf. "I don't want to do it anymore," she cried. "But you're not doing it right," he insisted. "Do it again, Dolly." She waded back out into the Gulf, while he yelled at her from the shore. "The crest. Do you know what I'm talking about? The crest. That's what you need to get into!"

As he spoke, a big one appeared in the distance. The father jumped into the water with his daughter, coaching her as it neared. "Now, now, NOW!"

Dahlia dove in time with the crest of the wave, and this time she was gone with surprising speed, thrilled at her success—"until I ran out of water and the wave dragged me by my face for 20 feet along the sand. My dad was screaming and jumping for joy. And my mom was screaming because blood was gushing down my face. I had a scab all week. But I knew I had pleased him."

With the full team of women now gathered around the table, Dahlia called the meeting to order. "The purpose of these new meetings is to meet weekly and discuss issues that impact the school, to learn about and participate in key decisions that impact the school, and to take on and expand the leadership roles in the school.

"To begin, let's reflect on what we've done so far." Dahlia passed around a two-page document that outlined different modes of decision-making. "OK, with a partner, pick any decision that's been made here, and tell me what it matches up to on the document."

The teachers went silent to read the handout, and the sounds and squeals of the children in the hallway beyond became audible again. *Making decisions is the heart of a partnership*, it read. *Unfortunately, many partners make decisions without understanding that there are different types of decisions, and a constant balancing act between maintaining control and sharing responsibility.*

Dahlia did her best to be patient as she waited for everyone to finish. She looked down to review her own notes in the margins of a section that outlined the five different types of decisions in an organization: authoritative, consultative, democratic, consensual, and delegated. *There are no right or wrong types of decision-making*, the handout concluded. *The type chosen must be weighed against the need for control, expediency, involvement, and responsibility. To be effective, your partnership needs to know which type of decision-making is best under which circumstances.*

Once everyone had finished reading, the teachers paired up and spoke in hushed tones. The two nearest to me spoke about a decision that was made without teacher input and then quickly censored themselves. "So we don't get fired," they whispered.

"OK," Dahlia interrupted after a few minutes. "What were some a-ha's?"

"It's easier to do democratic decision-making when you have time to do it," offered one teacher.

"Your location *vis à vis* a decision determines how you view it," said another.

"We need to become clear on what types of decisions are most essential for everyone to be involved in, and then stick to that," Berenice added.

"Everyone here belongs in this meeting," Dahlia responded to the young teachers in front of her. "We want everyone to be involved in decision-making. That doesn't mean everything is suddenly going to be decided by a majority vote—nor should it be. But it does mean that Kristin and I have heard you, and that we're really going to try to be more inclusive going forward. We're going to begin by asking you to help us think through a really important decision: whether we should transition next year to a full immersion school."

Over the break, this had been the question that consumed Kristin's thoughts. The first semester of Year One had been a blur, yet already she felt consumed with Year Two questions: Where would the school be located (they were too big to stay)? How would they round out their staff (which would double in size)? Adding another major question like whether or not to shift to full immersion seemed both unwise and unfair. And yet Kristin and the others had read the research, and watched their children swim in an omnipresent ocean of English outside the school walls. The implications were clear: an all-Spanish school would help the English speakers really learn the language, and help the Spanish speakers establish the strongest possible foundation from which to learn and grow.

In the past, a decision like this would have been made without teacher input. "What will you do if they don't honor your request to be included?" Molly's mother had asked her over the break. "I don't know," Molly answered. Yet here they were, on the first day, making space for a conversation about a major choice, and one that would directly affect her in her work. A good sign, she thought.

"We feel close to certain that making our preschool classrooms Spanish-only is the right decision," Kristin explained to the group. "But what about pre-K and kindergarten? That's where we need your help."

"This would mean a major shift in our culture," Dahlia added, "while we're still just getting started. *And* it would mean something else to work through at a time when we're set to double in size next year. How far should we take this transition?"

"It sounds like something that would be great for the kids," Berenice began. "But the logistics of this would need to be just right."

"I think it makes sense to envision big changes now, not incremental changes over many years," Molly added. "Especially if the research is suggesting that this is the better path." Similar voices of support followed.

Kristin and Dahlia looked at each other. "I'm still struggling with how far to go in taking this shift," Kristin said. "But I feel like I have a lot more information to go on, and I'm really grateful to you all for being so present in this conversation. Let's all keep thinking it through."

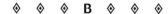

◊  ◊  ◊  **B**  ◊  ◊  ◊

It was a rainy morning on Bancroft's 88th day of the school year—January 17. A long line of parents and children formed outside the central office, signing in late.

Upstairs, Rebecca Lebowitz finalized her outline for the day so the children could see it as they arrived. Like every other day, that meant reading and writing all morning—first via a mini-lesson, then guided practice, and finally independent work.

> Reading: Good readers know they should stop and find the main point.
> Mini: Watch Ms. Lebowitz stop and find the main point.
> Writing: Good writers put their own thoughts in writing.
> Mini: Watch Ms. Schmidt do this in her writing.

As Ms. Lebowitz wrote, Ms. Schmidt sat at the desk they shared, grading a thick stack of math exams.

> Which unit is best for measuring the length of your classroom?
> a) Inches          b) Feet                    c) Miles
>
> Which object is about 10 feet high?
> a) A desk          b) A classroom wall      c) A mountain

Schmidt worked quickly through the stack, sipping her morning tea and, when I asked, speaking about the larger mood of the school. "I'm really proud of our school in a lot of ways—we do so much for the community and the kids we serve. But morale is really low right now. Teachers are not very happy, and I think it's because of all the emphasis on using data. Personally I think it's a good thing—it's easy to fall into the inertia of teaching without really knowing what's working—but I don't think the whole shift in approach was rolled out well."

As the first students began to arrive, Ms. Schmidt took a final sip of her tea. "What Ms. Reid doesn't see is that the problem isn't her or the program; it's the way folks were introduced to the program. People haven't received the training they need to do these new things well, and there isn't a clear overall sense of how all these new ideas fit together. It's just like good teaching—you need the scaffolding if you want to really take someone someplace new."

◇ ◇ ◇ **B** ◇ ◇ ◇

Downstairs, in the underground bunker that doubled as Bancroft's library, Zakiya Reid readied herself for the first open house of prospective families. She placed handouts on the seats of the six rectangular tables in front of her, and straightened the Styrofoam cups that stood next to the portable coffee maker. She centered the projector in front of the screen, focusing in on her opening slide: WELCOME TO BANCROFT ELEMENTARY SCHOOL.

Before any parents arrived, I asked how she was feeling about the start of the new semester. "Our data looks so much better than it has," she began. "I think some folks are starting to feel like maybe all this work is paying off. But I also worry about teachers like Lebowitz, who are visibly frustrated at the pace of change around here. Our teachers are beating themselves up," she added, as the first pairs of tentative mothers and fathers began to trickle in. "But I want them to see what they *have* done already. We're not starting from scratch here."

In some ways, Ms. Reid was right; a school like Bancroft, now in its third year of trying to shift to a more data-driven decision-making culture, was not starting from scratch. In other ways, however, the high degree of teacher turnover at Bancroft—12 teachers departed after her first year as principal, and 12 more after her second, representing almost half of the entire staff—made the process of trying to establish a cohesive culture much more difficult. "A lot of the teachers that left really needed to leave so we could start to do something different here," she explained. "But each year you also lose some of the people who you wish you could hold onto. I know we're going to lose Lebowitz and Schmidt eventually, but there isn't much I can do to hold onto them. They don't have any natural peer group here, and I know people say things like they want more involvement in governance—but that's not enough. It's just so much work, and some days, it feels harder to find the celebratory moments when you're part of such a large system, and so many of the decisions are not being made by you. But you have to not take things personally, and really focus."

Ms. Reid checked her watch; 15 minutes after the scheduled start time. Everyone that planned on attending was probably here by now. She looked out at the parents seated at the tables—16 adults, two with young children in tow—and welcomed them to Bancroft's first open house of the year. "Our school has 476 students—9% Asian, 14% Black, 5% White, and 72% Hispanic. And our vision is to be a student-centered, parent-involved, collaborative, community-based educational hub in which every student reaches their goals of high academic achievement."

Ms. Reid flipped through the slides of her presentation, periodically scanning the names each parent had written on their HELLO sticker. All the parents had written their first names only—all but one. Seated directly in front of the room, Zakiya Reid smiled at the serious African American mother, pen in hand, who wrote down every piece of information she had to share, and whose sticker served as its own personal calling card: YOLANDA HOOD.

## CHAPTER SEVEN

# Something Given

◊　◊　◊　**B**　◊　◊　◊

A S THE BANCROFT Elementary School bell rang for lunch—its sound the same shrill tone that has echoed in schools for generations—the students of room 121 jumped up to head downstairs after a long morning of reading and writing. Before they could line up, Ms. Lebowitz ordered them back in their seats. "Please fill out your exit slips before you leave," she said as she walked around the room, handing out small sheets of paper.

Ms. Lebowitz and Ms. Schmidt used the slips—short assessments of a key concept they had taught that morning—to gauge how well they had done their jobs. Usually no more than one or two questions, the slips took no more than 30 seconds to complete. Each worked quickly and made his or her way to the door. A few stopped off at the wall of emoticon plates to register changes in mood. Lourdes moved hers from Grumpy to Sleepy. Elliott upgraded himself to Fantastic. And Ms. Lebowitz moved quickly through the slips, pulling a few out where a misunderstanding had occurred, and dropping the rest immediately into the recycling bin.

Harvey, who had been in the "Chill Chair" when the bell rang, managed to escape to the coatroom before Ms. Lebowitz had ordered everyone to sit back down. He concealed himself behind the rows of hanging parkas, thrilled at the possibility that he'd evaded the usual routine.

The students filed out and down the stairwell to the lunchroom. As they did, Ms. Schmidt did a head count, returned to the classroom, and peered her head into the coatroom. "Hi there," she said, and Harvey emerged.

It had been a rough morning for him, although not in room 121. As a language immersion school, Bancroft's students split their day between an English-speaking and a Spanish-speaking classroom. As the year had gone on, Harvey had begun to trust his English-speaking teachers, and although he wasn't academically engaged, he was no longer rolling around the carpet. But the Spanish side was another story.

"He had a great morning here," Schmidt explained later. "But then he had a bad stretch next door. Our two rooms have different management styles, and I think everyone is feeling low on patience. It's such a large classroom, and there are so many needs. It's also a lot harder in the Spanish classroom because they have such fewer resources to work with. So I think what's happening now with him and his teachers there is all a result of that."

With everyone else out of the room, Ms. Schmidt and Harvey sat down at one set of desks. He kept his gaze focused downward, seemingly unaware of his teacher's presence.

"I want my mom to come pick me up," he said abruptly, eyes still on the desk in front of him.

"Why would you want to do that?" Ms. Schmidt replied.

"So I can plaaaaaayyyyyy," he explained in a mixture of mumbles and elongated syllables, his body contorting spasmodically, the chair unable to contain him. A moment later, he was on top of the desk. "In my rooooooooommmm."

"If you leave, we'd miss you," Ms. Schmidt said, prompting Harvey to hiss like a dragon in reply. He walked away from her, kicking furniture as he did.

"Would you like to play in here during recess?" she asked, fishing for something that could connect them.

"I can climb this wall," he replied.

"I don't think that's a good idea," she countered calmly. "This school is really old."

"I have a car."

"Is it one of those ones that shoots forward when you pull it back?"

Harvey returned to the desk where his teacher had continued to sit and placed his car on the desk between them. He moved it in circles, running his fingers over the stickers on the car's exterior. "I just want to go fast," he said.

"I think Ms. Lebowitz would love this car," Ms. Schmidt replied. "I'm going to write her a sticky note and ask her if this is the fastest car she's ever seen. What do you think she's going to say?"

"Yes!"

◈  ◈  ◈  **MV**  ◈  ◈  ◈

"Before we start today's professional development around the spring expeditions," Romey Pittman explained to the teachers before her, "I wonder if we can begin by having each person share a few words about a kid they're thinking about, and why."

"I'm thinking about Elan," said Molly, "who wasn't in school today—again. And I'm worrying about our kids who need our help the most, and who are here the least."

"I'm thinking about Freya," Berenice followed, "because I never think about Freya. All of our attention is usually wrapped up in the same 10–12 kids, and for someone like Freya, who's doing OK, I think we overlook them. That's what teachers did to me when I was a child."

As Romey listened to the teachers' responses, she thought about their bosses in the room next door. The January retreat at her farm was all about sustainability, but whereas the focus was environmental sustainability, Romey's personal emphasis was on helping Dahlia and Kristin ensure that the school *itself* was sustainable. She considered the pace of change they had established and wondered if it could be kept up for six months, let alone six years. And though they had explored that tension a little bit during the retreat, Romey knew more needed to be done.

In her mind, Mundo Verde was unintentionally creating an organizational model that relied on smart single women whose social lives would allow for crowded workweeks and little else (smart single men would have worked, too—it's just that there were so few at the elementary school level). Her job as a school designer was to help them chart a different course. But that job was easier said than done, and it had been hard to get uninterrupted time with Dahlia and Kristin. There was so much going on whenever she visited, and the very geography of the building—and the close quarters the two of them shared—dictated that decisions were bound to be made in relative isolation from the rest of the staff.

In Dahlia, Romey saw a leader with deep expertise and experience. And in Dahlia's staff, Romey saw young women who were being asked to do a lot without the benefit of the insights that their principal had acquired over the course of her career. Dahlia's professional path, like all professional paths, had been circuitous and dependent on a wide range of successes and failures. How do you build a great school, Romey wondered, when the majority of the teachers, even a staff as capable and effective as this one, haven't had enough formative experiences themselves?

Over the course of her career, and throughout her time as a school designer for Expeditionary Learning (EL), Romey had seen that success looked different in different places. That was why EL described its relationship with the schools in its network as a partnership; each school decided how they wanted to use EL practices and what they wanted to emphasize, in exchange for agreeing to partner with EL, represent the EL identity, and gain access to the network's intellectual property, its school designers, and its professional development.

At the center of that shared identity was the wisdom of a veteran public school teacher from Massachusetts named Ron Berger. "To build a new culture, a new ethic," he wrote in his book *An Ethic of Excellence*, "you need a focal point—a vision—to guide the direction for reform. The particular spark I try to share as a catalyst is a passion for beautiful student work and developing conditions that can make this work possible.

"I have a hard time thinking about a quick fix for education," Berger continues, "because I don't think education is broken. Some schools are very good; some are not. Those that are good have an ethic, a culture, which supports and compels students to try and to succeed. Those schools that are not need a lot more than new tests and new mandates. They need to build a new culture and a new ethic."

To build a new ethic at a school, of course—whether it's a months-old charter school or a decades-old neighborhood school—one must begin *somewhere*. And Berger believes high-quality student work is the logical place to start. "Work of excellence is transformational," he writes. "Once a student sees that he or she is capable of excellence, that student is never quite the same. We can't first build the students' self-esteem and then focus on their work. It is through their own work that their self-esteem will grow. If schools assumed they were going to be assessed by the quality of student behavior and work evident in the hallways and classrooms—rather than on test scores—the enormous energy poured into test preparation would be directed instead toward improving student work, understanding, and behavior. And so instead of working to build clever test-takers, schools would feel compelled to spend time building thoughtful students and good citizens."

The clearest manifestation of Berger's belief in the power of student work was the EL belief in the power of expeditions—multi-week explorations of a topic that involved not just original research, but also a culminating project that was presented to the public. Across the EL network, however, there were very few examples of expeditions being done with children as young as the three-, four-, and five-year-olds at Mundo Verde.

Consequently, Romey had felt that the first-semester expedition on water had its moments, but trying to successfully coordinate such a complex project while also trying to negotiate the unique chaos of a brand-new school's first few months of operation was, to say the least, challenging. Because the staff were so smart and so committed, they'd managed to make it work in spite of everything that was conspiring to derail them. But everyone, Romey included, had much higher hopes for the second semester.

As she packed up her book bag to head home after another long workday, Berenice Pernalete looked around her room at the remnants of their first-semester expedition. In one corner, a large colorful canvas explained the rationale behind the project itself. She and her co-teacher, Laura Rainey, had worked until 9:00 P.M. most nights in the weeks leading up to the public presentation of their work, trying to make everything perfect. They'd both felt the sting of disappointment afterward when the parents didn't show much appreciation. Were they not aware how hard it was for them to create these things? Didn't they see that those vocabulary cards had each been hand-drawn?

Occasionally, moments like this would arrive and Berenice would feel the full weight of her work and how hard it was. Yet she felt much less burned out than her colleagues. Perhaps it was because of the fact that, unlike many of them, she'd experienced real professional hardship before.

It wasn't long after beginning her career at a public school in Manhattan—P.S. 165, all the way up on 108th Street—that Berenice first found herself wondering if she was meant to be a teacher. The endless days of teaching 30 children, all by herself, had left her feeling isolated and devoid of community. "I felt like my brain was atrophying," she explained to me one afternoon. "I was getting dumber."

So Berenice began to imagine a very different life for herself. Part of that was personal; she was married at the time, to a struggling writer who was waiting tables. "I was supporting him. I believed in him and wanted him to succeed but after a while I felt like he wasn't moving forward, and that I was letting my passion slip away because I had this responsibility with an adult. That marked the decline of our marriage."

The other part was professional; and it led Berenice to leave education altogether in order to work with two documentary filmmakers in D.C. A few years later, however, the irreplaceable lure of teaching returned—and the daily possibility of changing the life trajectory of a young person. When she heard about Mundo Verde, she knew it was the right point of re-entry.

Berenice was still sure it *was* the right place for her to be. But that didn't change the fact that one semester in, despite the school's clear value for bilingualism, her students didn't feel as accountable for learning as they did in the English classroom. Their change in attitude was palpable, and what it said to her was, "I'm in Spanish; this isn't as important." She knew she wasn't doing anything wrong, but the fact that a majority of the students in the English classroom were being spoken to in their own language made everything easier.

Berenice thought about the possibilities inherent in the new expedition as she rode the train back to her group house. Sometimes her school was not as organized as she'd like, but everyone's attitude was so supportive.

She thought of Dahlia, and how inspired she felt by her principal's passion. She'd also watched what happened when Dahlia acted out of that passion. The frustration she felt was very visible, and Berenice had seen how some of the younger teachers took it so personally. "C'mon now," she'd think. "Let's get some perspective, ladies." Maybe it was because both women were Latina, and because both were coming out of some difficult personal times. But if Dahlia can do it, Berenice thought as she exited the train, I can do it. *"Si la puerta está cerrada, toca la ventana":* If the door is closed, knock on the window.

◇  ◇  ◇  **B**  ◇  ◇  ◇

Valerie Flores arrived to school on a Wednesday in mid-February, knowing it was the day she tended to her considerable pile of paperwork and administrative follow-up. Several months had passed since she and Ms. Lebowitz had initiated the process of getting Harvey evaluated, and they were still months away from completing it.

Flores had completed her part—three classroom observations of Harvey and a detailed interview with his family. But the larger bureaucracy of the system always slowed everything down, and Ms. Flores had been in the profession long enough to know that these sorts of efforts to provide additional supports had both happy and unhappy endings. There was that young teenage girl from Mexico, the one who'd been in the country about six months, first working on farms in Alabama, and then slowly making her way toward a big sister in D.C. But then she and the sister got into a huge physical fight, and the police came, and the girl entered foster care, undocumented and pregnant. Flores took her to the doctor once, and discovered that she had never been to one in her life; she was terrified by everything she saw there—from the needles to the baby monitor machine. Valerie tracked her father down in Mexico, in some small village with a single phone he had to drive to in order to speak with a lawyer. She listened to the tired voice on the other end of the line, a surge of mixed emotions rising up in her as he agreed to sign over all rights so his daughter could have a better life and become an official ward of the state. But then she had her baby, and within six months the baby was removed from her care. She was shaking it. He must be two by now, Flores thought. I hope he's found a home.

It was too soon to know if Harvey's path would end well or poorly, but she had success stories to pull from as well. Her first year at Bancroft, she began working with a third-grade student who was regularly walking out of class, fighting with kids, and yelling at teachers. Flores worked hard that year to get his mother on board with getting him evaluated, but the mom, for whatever reason, wasn't ready to hear that message; it bounced right off her. So Flores approached the problem a different way, and began working with a classroom teacher the mother trusted. The teacher echoed the message back to the family, and by year's end, the boy had been both evaluated and held back. He ran for student government the following year—promising pizza and ice cream for everyone. "Those sorts of things aren't measured in our performance reviews," Flores pointed out. "But think of the growth in self-confidence that boy experienced! And now this child who had been such a distraction was reading on grade-level."

Flores picked up the phone to call central office and get a status report on Harvey's outside assessment by a psychologist. "What we really need," she told me as she waited for someone to pick up, "is comprehensive training for all of our teachers, not just the ones who are officially designated as "Special Ed." That would be a game-changer. That would enable all of our teachers to work with every kind of kid. That's one of the biggest challenges for our teachers; they're not getting that sort of training in their schooling. It's about managing the curriculum, not managing all of those unmet social needs. But we're all counselors in this work, whether we want to be or not. And that requires us to rely on a different sort of data."

When it comes to evaluating the overall health of a school—whether you're a prospective parent or a state agency—which data are most relevant, and why?

Since 2002, federal policy in America has provided a clear answer: what matters most are a child's scores on standardized exams in reading and math. Since then, schools have adjusted their schedules and priorities accordingly, resulting in a modern landscape of public education in which many children experience daily deep dives into the intricacies of numbers and letters—and barely skim the surface of anything else.

The willingness of policymakers—and, by extension, the general public—to judge schools based on this single metric of success is one of the more surreal features of modern American school reform. By comparison, the private sector has long since moved away from using net income as a company's sole benchmark, and many businesses have adopted a "balanced scorecard" approach that features both financial and non-financial metrics, and both inputs and outcomes. In doing so, these businesses have rightly heeded the 1976 warnings of social psychologist Donald Campbell, who said: "The more any quantitative social indicator is used for social decision-making, the more subject it will be to corruption pressures and the more apt it will be to distort and corrupt the social processes it is intended to monitor."

This insight, which has come to be known as "Campbell's Law," does not mean measurement has no place in organizational improvement. It does mean, however, that if policymakers are serious about evaluating whether or not schools are successful, they need to go a lot deeper than reading and math scores. As the Fordham Institute's Kathleen Porter-Magee puts it, "If we value learning in other areas, we need to measure it. And that doesn't mean simply adding testing hours but rather being more deliberate and creative about the assessments we administer and the content they measure."[1]

Despite the illogic of the current accountability system in American schools, there weren't sufficiently loud cries of protest against it until recently. Over the course of the year I spent with Mundo Verde and Bancroft, however, pockets of resistance began to pop up in different parts of the country, suggesting a growing consensus that it was time for a change—although what to, exactly, was still anyone's guess. In Maryland, the superintendent of the state's largest district of schools called for a three-year moratorium[2] on standardized tests; in Washington, one school's decision to boycott its state tests ended up spreading to other schools and communities;[3] and in Texas, a proposed Senate bill sought to significantly reduce the number of state standardized tests students must pass to graduate.[4]

In all three places—and many more across the country—what had
changed was a growing willingness to publicly acknowledge that standardized tests, when used as a metric for high-stakes decision-making,
do not align well with the latest research into how people learn; that
they prevent adults from measuring higher-level thinking in children;
and, most important, that there are better ways to evaluate student
learning and growth. As Montgomery County Superintendent Joshua
Starr put it, policymakers need to "stop the insanity" of evaluating
teachers and students via a formula that is based on "bad science."
Starr's critique was echoed by Seattle teacher Jesse Hagopian. "We've
been raising our voices about this deeply flawed test for a long time,"
he explained to the *Wall Street Journal*. But now that his district was
planning to use it for evaluations, Hagopian and other educators like
him had "drawn our line in the sand."[5] And as Texas education com-
missioner Robert Scott put it, student testing had become a "perver-
sion of its original intent," and educators needed to do whatever they
could to "reel it back" in the future.

Of course, even today the American test obsession maintains a firm
hold on our collective psyche, and with Common Core assessments
around the corner, we're a long way off from the model of a country
like Finland—in which there are no national tests and all student assessments are devised and administered locally by teachers. But what
seems clear is that a new sort of idea is gaining strength in education
circles. And as Malcolm Gladwell explained in his bestselling book *The
Tipping Point*, "Ideas and products and messages and behaviors spread
just like viruses do. When we're trying to make an idea or attitude or
product tip, we're trying to change our audience in some small yet
critical respect: we're trying to infect them, sweep them up in our epidemic, convert them from hostility to acceptance."[6]

Policy debates aside, the most relevant question for educators like
Rebecca Schmidt and Rebecca Lebowitz was not whether testing itself
was good or bad, but which data about their students were most relevant to their own growth and development. And what was clear at
a school like Bancroft was that the faculty, largely along generational
lines, had very different understandings of what that word—data—
augured for their profession.

For younger teachers like Schmidt and Lebowitz, "data-driven decision-making" was all they'd known in their careers. As a result, although they expressed frustration with the ubiquity of the tests, it felt natural for them to consistently assess their students' comprehension levels, and to evaluate their own effectiveness against those numbers. I could see the appeal on those days I observed them reviewing the results of a math exam, and drilling down on each question to diagnose a particular concept that may have been challenging for an individual student, or perhaps even a majority of the class. In these instances, their use of data was both surgical and insightful.

As useful as the numbers were for a subject like math, however, Lebowitz and Schmidt found them considerably less valuable for a subject like reading and writing, which relied on a more fluid and overlapping set of skills and dispositions. Consequently, for teachers whose careers pre-dated the current data obsession, it was easy to see why the word had come to take on a negative connotation. "Anyone that has been in D.C. as long as I have sees how urgently we need reform," said Toni Conklin, a 19-year veteran educator at Bancroft. "But there's such a lack of balance—it's all about reading and math. I feel like we've swung the pendulum too far. And now there's something essential that's missing."

◇  ◇  ◇  **B**  ◇  ◇  ◇

Every Friday afternoon, Bancroft's third-graders would crowd into room 121 to deliver shout outs before scattering to start their weekends. During the day, the grade was split evenly between the English and Spanish classrooms; this was the only time all 60 of them tried to fit into the same room. Desks that were ordinarily one or another student's home base had to be shared, and the amount of body heat being let off always gave this part of the week—even during the winter months—a stuffy, sticky feel.

"It's been a long week," Ms. Lebowitz said on a Friday in late February. "We've done a lot of work and it's nice to come together before we all head home. Who's got some shout outs?"

"I've got one," Ms. Schmidt replied. "I want to give a shout out to Harvey, who's been super focused in writing. He has really interesting stories and I've been excited to see him working so hard on his personal narratives."

"I want to give a shout out to Ms. Lebowitz," said Lourdes, "because all I had today was a skinny jacket and she gave me a scarf."

"I'm giving a shout out to Ernesto," said a girl named Mya, "because he's been writing some great stories."

"I want to give a shout out to Harvey," said Elliott, prompting another boy to protest. "That's his third time!" the boy pleaded. But Harvey was always, it seemed, at the center of everyone's thoughts.

"At the beginning of the year," Elliott continued, "he was really mean to me. But now he's nice."

"Alright, everyone," Ms. Lebowitz announced. "Let's do our song."

The students started zipping up their backpacks and shifting in their seats. "Who rocks the house?" a young girl yelled abruptly.

"Bancroft rocks the house!" the class thundered back in unison.

"Who rocks the house?"

"Bancroft rocks the house. And when Bancroft rocks the house, they rock it all the way down!"

"Have a great weekend, everyone," yelled Ms. Lebowitz.

Five minutes later, everyone was gone.

## CHAPTER EIGHT

# The Dance of the Waiting Lists

YOLANDA HOOD CHECKED her list of inspections and looked at her watch. Three more buildings to go. The timing was going to be tight.

Yolanda had been a building inspector for the city since 2005. Each day she'd get a list of properties—usually between 10 and 15. The rest was up to her. She had always loved the freedom of her job, and the space it afforded her to decide the order and pace of her day. Now that Hunter was almost school age, she loved something else: the opportunity to attend all the different charter school open houses—many of which were scheduled for the middle of a workday.

Yolanda walked off the perimeter of a public patio outside a neighborhood bar; someone had complained that it encroached upon the public sidewalk. She wrote down the measurements, snapped a few pictures, and raced back to the office to pull up the allowable dimensions. She had 30 minutes before her 25th—and final—open house of the spring.

Twenty-five minutes later, as she left the office to hop in her car and drive across town, Yolanda wondered how people could stand working inside all day long, day after day. She drove past a shoe store with a giant SALE sign outside and thought briefly about stopping. For years, Yolanda had been purchasing tennis shoes for her son that wouldn't be worn by him for years. "Hunter has shoes until he wears a size 10 men's," she told me one day. "If I see a deal, I won't pass it up."

Yolanda arrived at the seven-year-old school—mature by local standards—that was named after a pioneering African American educator, civil rights activist, and onetime adviser to President Franklin Delano Roosevelt: Mary McLeod Bethune. She entered the building. No sign of metal detectors; good. The other day, she had visited a school where she had to walk through one. "I didn't leave right then and there because I didn't want to be rude," she said.

She sat in the front row and pulled out a pen and paper to take notes she would enter in her spreadsheet later that night. Yolanda had arrived that morning feeling skeptical about the school, which was overwhelmingly African American. Diversity was important to her, and when 98% of the children were the same color as her son, that wasn't diversity. But as she listened to the bow-tied principal speak passionately about the school and its program, she found herself getting lured in.

*Spanish immersion program,* she wrote. *Creative curriculum. No more than 20 students in each class. Ratio is 10:1 there are 2 teachers in each class: a lead and an assistant.*

Yolanda always paid attention to the people that represented the school at an open house. In particular she was looking to see if any parents of current students were on hand. "I need a school where your parents are your top cheerleaders," she explained. "If they're not, then what kind of team do you have?"

Yolanda had always known that whatever school Hunter attended in the fall was going to be getting a package deal. "I plan to take with me the best ideas I've heard from the other places. A lot of folks just aren't putting in the time—they're just going for the winners. I'm more attracted to the idea of helping to *build* a winning school. And that's possible right now in this day and age."

The principal finished his presentation and opened it up for questions. Yolanda waited a moment out of deference to the other prospective families in the room. When they hesitated, she jumped in.

"Can children bring cupcakes to school on their birthday?"

"Of course," the principal said.

Yolanda nodded. Nothing makes friends better than mommy bringing in cupcakes.

"Are your teachers CPR certified?"

"Every one."

Yolanda scribbled in her notebook, surprised at what she was feeling. Ordinarily, she viewed most of what she heard at these events with a healthy dose of skepticism. "If I could, I would hypnotize 90% of people to tell the truth," she told me. "So much more would come out than what actually comes out." But something about this principal—about the way he spoke so knowledgeably about his students and their strengths and weaknesses—made her wonder if this was the one.

Later that night, Yolanda sat at her dining room table and updated her spreadsheet. "What do you like?" read the header of one category. *EVERYTHING!* She wrote. "Overall rank," read the final column. *1.*

Fred Solowey arrived at the front doors of Bancroft Elementary School in late March with two very different things to drop off. In one hand, he held fresh copies of *Bancroft Stories,* a collection of life stories from fellow parents he had organized and edited in order to bring the community closer together. In the other, he held a confidential report that had consumed the previous three weeks of his time, and which was guaranteed to drive that same community apart.

*The Crisis at Bancroft Elementary School,* it read. *By Fred J. Solowey.* Just underneath was a lead sentence in oversized font: "The fact that 12 of the 22 teachers I interviewed may not return to Bancroft next year only begins to explain why I refer to the situation at Bancroft as being a crisis."

As Fred walked down the hallway between the school's front doors and the principal's office, he felt the irony—and the tragedy—of delivering a report with such a foreboding headline. As PTA president he had been a part of the selection committee that hired Zakiya Reid three years earlier (although she was not his preferred choice); and as a longtime labor activist and communications expert, he had been the one, way back when, to first give the school its slogan: *Nuestra Escuela.*

"The slogan is meant to reflect the message that 'Our School' means we're all stakeholders here," he explained. "It belongs to the children, it belongs to the parents, and it belongs to the community. Any person in this community can say 'That's my school.' And every kid can have pride that this is my school. It just seemed simple and it seemed right. The only way you have a great school is to have all of those folks combined and working together."

Fred Solowey had lived among all of those folks, in the Mount Pleasant neighborhood, for more than 20 years. A sixty-something father of one with neatly combed salt-and-pepper hair and glasses, he spent most of those years paying very little attention to public schools. "I didn't have a kid; I wasn't a teacher," he said. "But then we adopted Ben, and I realized I had a great predisposition for wanting to go to our neighborhood school. Now Ben is about to head off to middle school, and I've been really happy overall with his experience here. I recently took a bunch of the Bancroft kids bowling for his birthday, and there was a kid of African parents, a kid of Caribbean parentage, two kids from Central America, a Vietnamese kid, and a couple of White kids. I sat there at the bowling alley and looked at his group of friends and felt like he was really a citizen of the unfolding America, and of the world. That's who he's becoming. He has a class sensitivity that he wouldn't have if he went to Sidwell Friends."

Fred's belief in the importance of public education had prompted him to write an open letter to President Obama in the *Washington Post* after it was reported that the First Family chose Sidwell—a prestigious D.C. private school—for their daughters because there weren't any viable options in DCPS. "Dear President Obama," he wrote, "Your daughters would have thrived, received a bilingual education and gotten the invaluable social education not possible at most private schools. Through interaction with children from the many immigrant and mostly working-class families, they would have been as enriched as my son, now in his fifth year at Bancroft, has been. . . . I urge you to spend some time at my son's school. It would be good for you and good for America."

In the two years following the writing of that letter and the decision to step down as PTA president, Fred had tried to "stay out of the picture. But I got drawn back into things with the Bancroft stories project. I saw it as a model of community schools—a lot more to keep families tied in. The whole idea of this was to send a message to that whole population—you're important, your learning is important, your role in the lives of your kids is important."

Then, while working on the stories, Fred started getting approached by different teachers at Bancroft. "Because they knew me and trusted me, they asked me to do something. They said, 'This place is going to hell this year; the conditions are terrible.'" So I did those interviews.

"I burned a lot of midnight oil in those three weeks of interviewing. I was appalled as a parent and as someone who thinks teaching is really important. What I found was a pattern of intimidation against teachers, and a fear of retribution against anyone who dared to disagree with the principal's approach. All working people deserve respectful treatment and they weren't getting it. The war on unions has had the effect of undermining the status of educators. Yeah there are some bad teachers—and some get burned out—but every teacher can learn to improve. To pretend that teachers can be given magic bullets by their genius administrators and overcome all these larger social issues is myopic and outrageous—and stupid.

"I just hope a sense of balance will get restored. The charter stuff is gaining in power. We still need neighborhood schools."

At 6:30 P.M. on the night of the 2nd Annual D.C. Parent Choice Forum, the streets outside the All Souls Church on 16th and Harvard were typically congested, each driver inching his or her way home in the syrupy evening commute. Karen Copeland, walking at equal speed with the gridlocked cars, entered the church and headed to the basement, where volunteers were arranging the last of the folding chairs and uncorking the last of the bottles of wine. While organizers waited for the final stragglers to arrive, she listened in as a group of parents—mostly women, with some men—sipped their drinks and swapped war stories.

"I've decided my top three factors are proximity, size, and not being the 'only' anything at the school."

"Knowing why you choose a school is going to be key to knowing why you stay."

"We've been at this great preschool, but because it's only for three- and four-year olds, everyone knows they're only there for two years and no one really invests in building a sense of community there."

"The best way to get into a tough in-boundary school is by switching mid-year."

"Make sure you ask to see the nontraditional classrooms. Otherwise they'll only show you what they want you to see."

While the parents chatted, Karen watched a woman place a stack of thick blue books on the table in front of her. *DC School Chooser 2012–2013. A K–12 Guide to Finding a Great School for Your Child.* When parents slid in front of her to grab a copy, another mother leaned toward her and whispered, "Make sure you get one of those. That book is like your bible."

Karen grabbed a copy and opened it up. She scanned the table of contents.

*Five Steps to Choosing a School.*

*DC School Chooser Workbook.*

*School Profiles.*

She skipped to the last section and found page after page of schools, arranged alphabetically and by grade level, with uniform descriptions: private, public, or charter; address and available bus lines; school size, uniform policy, income level, diversity profile, languages taught, re-enrollment rates. At the top, each school received an oversized five-star rating based on its test scores from the previous year; the higher the scores, the higher the rating. "My name is Kelli Anderson, and I'm the Community Outreach Coordinator for GreatSchools," the book-stacking woman explained. "My job is to make your search easier and more informed, so take my card and call or email me anytime."

I don't know how many parents took Kelli up on her offer, but the impact her organization had had on prospective parents in D.C. is unmistakable. At the Charter Schools Expo in January, GreatSchools books were ubiquitous. And although outliers like Yolanda Hood had decided to construct their own versions of the Chooser, at every open house I attended parents clutched heavily highlighted, dog-eared copies.

What all of them were in search of was the same secret code Karen Copeland had first described to me: how to determine what a healthy, high-functioning learning environment actually *looked like*, and required. And what all of them were finding as the first lottery dates neared was that the recipe for school success is an elusive set of ingredients that is extremely difficult to convey simply and clearly—something Bill Jackson knows all too well.

Back in 1998, when the concept of school choice was still in its infancy, Jackson founded GreatSchools as a way to harness the potential of the Internet to help parents become more effectively involved in their children's education. Today, GreatSchools is the country's leading source of information on school performance, with listings of 200,000 public and private schools serving students from preschool through high school, a cache of nearly 1 million parent ratings and reviews, a website that receives more than 44 million visitors a year, and, in a few cities like Washington, D.C., employees like Kelli to provide real-time support.

The success of GreatSchools stems in large part from Jackson's prescient anticipation of the rise of school choice. Yet its growth owes as much to something Jackson couldn't have anticipated: the passage of No Child Left Behind, and the ways that legislation, almost overnight, shifted conversations about schooling away from a belief that the core components of a school couldn't be measured, and toward the idea that it's possible to measure schools solely by their students' scores on state reading and math tests.

The GreatSchools ratings system followed suit, allowing Jackson to compare schools in a way that was easy and unambiguous. And yet even though the books Kelli Anderson was handing out were still using the old rating formula, Jackson and his colleagues were already in search of a new, more balanced, replacement.

What else should a ratings system incorporate, Jackson wondered? And what are the core ingredients parents could look for—and demand—as a way to drive improvement across all schools? To answer those questions, Jackson hired Samantha Olivieri, a former educator and self-styled "data diva," and charged her with leading the process of devising a more balanced ratings system for schools.

As Olivieri explained it to me, the new system reflects an observation that is both simple and significant: what makes or breaks a school is not its performance on a single state test, but the quality of its overall culture. "We want parents to find not just a great school, but also the best possible fit for their child—and that's tricky. It's a lot harder to measure qualitative data in a way that's consistent and useful."

Nonetheless, Olivieri and her colleague devised a five-part portrait of school culture:

1. Robust teacher support;
2. Active family engagement;
3. Supportive environmental conditions;
4. Strong social and emotional student growth; and
5. A school-wide climate of high expectations.

For some of the categories, Olivieri knew that schools already collect quantitative data that can provide a useful snapshot: student attendance, for example, or student re-enrollment and faculty absenteeism rates. For others, an entity like GreatSchools is left to rely on qualitative measures that different schools and districts must choose to collect and share, like attitudinal surveys of students, teachers, and parents, or more specific information about their programmatic features and what makes them distinctive.

"We're trying different things out right now," Olivieri explained, "and we're searching for what will be both credible and actionable. Part of the challenge is that most parents do not have a depth of experience on which to rely. When people rate a restaurant on Yelp, they do so after attending hundreds of restaurants. But that's not generally how it works with schools; for most of us, the range of reference is quite limited.

"I understand that the phrase 'data-driven' has taken on a negative tone because of the way it's been misused in the past," she added. "But that doesn't mean we should swing back in the other direction. The data *do* tell us something. And it's true that education is not a field that can easily measure the most valuable outcomes. It's a challenge—but it's an exciting challenge, and I'm excited to see what we can learn—and how we can help."

By the time the Forum officially began, at 7:00 P.M., 40 adults were in attendance, all of them facing a panel of five parents whose children were already enrolled in either a district or a charter school. At the back of the room, strangely separate from the conversation, several principals of area schools sat behind small desks with handouts of their schools and programs.

Each mother on the panel held court for a few minutes describing the things they loved most about their child's school.

"I love that imagination is an explicit priority."

"I don't care as much about numbers and letters at this age—what matters most to me is that my school really values social and emotional growth."

"I love being able to attend my neighborhood school and all that it brings. And something you should all think about is the scale that a district can provide—my son's school has full-time gym and art teachers. You won't find that at most of the charters, especially the ones that are only a few years old."

When the room opened up to questions, the growing worries of the parents colored every one that was asked.

"I was exactly where all of you were a year ago," said one encouraging veteran, "and all I can tell you is that almost everyone I know got into at least one school that they felt good about it. This thing they call 'The Dance of the Waiting Lists' is real, and it lasts from March to mid-September, but as long as you can deal with the uncertainty, there's so much movement between schools that your child is almost guaranteed to get in somewhere good."

A principal in the back stood up and spoke. "I can tell you right now that if you travel during the summer, be sure you have a working phone number on file with us. I go through that list one by one, and it goes quickly."

The meeting ended, and Karen refilled her Dixie cup with warm white wine. She perused the school tables at the back and picked up everything they had to offer.

"I know it's stressful," someone said to her, "but really—if you're in this room, your kids will be fine."

◊   ◊   ◊   **MV**   ◊   ◊   ◊

As Molly Howard finished her morning coffee, she shoved the final pieces of her homemade frog costume into her backpack. Today was the day she officially kicked off the spring expedition, and she wanted everything to be perfect.

Molly hopped on her bike and rode the short distance to the school, past the lobbyists and the consultants and the local residents walking their dogs. Early arrivals filed past her as she dismounted. It was a full hour before the start of the school day, but for a small number of children whose parents had no other options, their day started as early as Molly's did. By the time it ended, at 6:00 P.M., these children would have spent almost 11 hours away from home.

Molly put on her costume and reviewed the script one last time. A short while later, while her students sat expectantly on the rug, she hopped in as Francesca the Frog.

"Hear the live-ly song of the frog in yon-der pond," sang Dahlia, skipping just ahead of her daughter, the frog. "Croak croak, crickety croak."

The children's eyes widened at the sight of such unexpected visitors. Stephen fell backward theatrically and then shot back up. Albert yelped.

"I want a pair of wings like a bird!" Francesca whined.

"Frogs don't need wings," her mother replied.

"Then how about giving me a fin like a fish?"

"Francesca, you don't need a fin like a fish."

Dahlia turned to the students, rapt with attention, and addressed them directly for the first time. "Children, I'm so happy you're here. I'm going to have Francesca come back in a month, and I need you to help me convince her of just how special her frog body actually is, and how special her parts are. Can you help me?"

"Yesssss!!!!!!"

For weeks, Molly had been preparing for the official kickoff of the spring expedition, when she would unveil the particular challenge of what the students would be studying. "They're going to study frogs for the next four or five weeks," she explained as she changed back out of her costume, "and then apply what they've learned to other animals. The goal is to help them understand why animals look the way they look. And by the time it's done they'll realize that the expedition isn't actually about frogs; it's about animal adaptations."

Back in September, Molly felt overwhelmed in her efforts to construct an engaging expedition, identify clear and challenging learning targets, *and* connect the work to state standards. But this time, she had a much clearer sense of where she wanted the children to end up, and the learning targets to prove it.

"The process of learning shouldn't be a mystery to students," Expeditionary Learning explains in its toolkit for teachers. "Learning targets provide them with tangible goals that they can understand and work toward. The student becomes the main actor in assessing and improving his or her learning."

Berenice Pernalete had been hard at work, too. In her classroom, the students would be studying Monarch butterflies, and learning more about the efforts conservationists had taken to ensure that the population could sustain itself in a changing world. "My apologies, children," she muttered in Spanish on the day of her classroom kickoff. She was dressed as an old man, with a mustache and beard made out of black construction paper and an oversized sombrero. "It's just that I came from very far away—from the Michoacán region.

"I came here because I have a problem. There are people cutting down trees in Michoacán. Oh, dear friends, as a result when our poor friends the Monarch butterflies travel from here, at the end of summer, and make their way to Michaocán, they have no place to live.

"All of us can work together to help so that no more trees are cut down. Do you want to help me do this?"

"¡Ssiiiiiiiii!!!"

While her teachers kicked off their spring expeditions, Dahlia Aguilar was eyeing the spring report card, and still trying to implement an evaluation system for her teachers and students. "I see teachers here who are getting feedback, but they're not being evaluated at all," she said amidst the quotidian chaos of her office. "We hired folks with a certain disposition, and a desire for continuous improvement. But what happens when we double our staff next year? How can we make sure everyone feels like they're able to really hone their craft?"

As she spoke, a large book in front of her represented the other immediate challenge. "Objectives for Development & Learning," it read, under the header Teaching Strategies GOLD. Inside, the book's opening pages outlined a comprehensive assessment system for the youngest grades, "based on 38 research-based objectives that include predictors of school success and are aligned with the Common Core State Standards, state early learning guidelines, and the Head Start Child Development and Early Learning Framework.

"Our state-of-the-art, interactive options," the authors explained, "enable teachers and administrators to run reports with just a few clicks of the mouse. Built-in support for every type of learner, embedded professional development support, and meaningful ways to involve families are just a few of the features that make our assessment solutions truly unique."

It sounded ideal, and when Dahlia first heard of the GOLD system, she imagined her teachers easily downloading either whole-class or individual child reports, or generating a Development & Learning report that could be shared with parents, and even provide suggested activities for families who wanted to reinforce what was happening at the school. And she took great comfort in the knowledge that the skills her school would be assessing reflected social and emotional growth as much as academic progress.

What she had discovered, however, was that the idea of GOLD and the reality of its implementation in a first-year school were two very different things. Indeed, it was almost time for report cards again, and yet teachers had not yet been trained in how to use the online interface of GOLD, and the template for the school's overall report card itself was still very much a work in progress. Dahlia imagined all that information about her children—nearly a year's worth—that had yet to be codified, and knew that it was slowly slipping through her school's figurative fingers.

A few days earlier, Dahlia learned that the Public Charter School Board had revoked the charters of a few city schools. "I don't ever want that to be us," she said. "It makes you ask yourself, 'What happened? What could they have done differently?'"

"I remember from my days in DCPS that mandates would always be coming down from central office, a lot of which you wouldn't necessarily like. But your task as a building principal was to honor the policy mandates *and* maintain your preferred focus. As a charter school, we have no such tension; we can do whatever we want, as long as we get results. But the amount of things that have to be done, and the number of decisions that have to be made—I guess you can see how a school could have the best intentions, but make a few too many wrong decisions, and then boom! It's over."

◈   ◈   ◈   **B**   ◈   ◈   ◈

Rebecca Schmidt exited Rock Creek Park and ran past the school toward home. It was dusk; usually it would be darker when she hit this final stretch, but with the D.C. Marathon just a few weeks away, she had started running less, and resting more.

As April neared, Rebecca knew that the schedule would become even more consumed with testing than it already was.

In September they'd administered the first of the A-Net math assessments, as per DCPS instructions. In November, the students went through another round of A-Net, and the first round of the Dynamic Indicators of Basic Early Literacy Skills, or DIBELS—a standardized, individually administered measure of early reading skills. In January and March, they did additional rounds of A-Net and DIBELS. In April, they'd spend two weeks administering the DC-CAS. And then in May, they'd give a test called Access to the 45 or so children in third grade who were designated as English-language learners, and a final round of A-Net and DIBELS.

By the time the final exam of the year rolled around, in June— a teacher- or school-created final math assessment—it was hard not to feel discouraged by the amount of time the children spent being assessed, and the duplicative nature of the tests themselves. And for whatever reason, this year—her fifth at Bancroft—was increasingly feeling like the breaking point for Rebecca Schmidt.

"When I feel the worst is when I feel like I can't fix or improve something—or that no matter what I do, things are going to get worse," she told me. "I've been feeling that way too many times at school this year—filling out documents, or feeling that no matter how hard we work, what we do doesn't ever seem to be enough. We lecture at our families in so many ways about reading to their children more, but a lot of our parents work all the time. Most have at least two jobs. Lately I feel like I'm just adding to their guilt. I don't know what else to do or how else to talk to them. And there is so much that needs to be done!

"Everything we hear is 'differentiate, differentiate, differentiate'—
and then we give them this one high-stakes test in April? With a single
metric for evaluating both us and the school? C'mon."

The last time Schmidt remembered feeling this frustrated was during the "Snowmageddon" blizzard of 2010. She had planned a much-
needed San Francisco vacation. Then the snow came, and she was
stuck in her apartment for four days. Then the airline canceled her
flight. "I have to get out of here," she thought. *"I have to get out."*

So Rebecca Schmidt spent several hours digging out her car, found
another flight, and after four hours spent idling on the tarmac, her
plane took off and she arrived in San Francisco.

The weekend that followed was one of the happiest of her life—
no plans, just wandering around, feeling free, and eating burritos in
Golden Gate Park. She wanted to feel that sense of levity again. And as
she took off her running shoes, she realized for the first time that when
her co-teacher left for grad school, she would be leaving, too.

"We're going to spend some time today talking about a new topic on
probability," Ms. Lebowitz began on a late March morning. "It's called
combinations. What's a combination?"

"It's like a lock," said Lourdes.

"It's when you put things together," Elliott added.

On the whiteboard behind their teacher, the students of room 121
read the following: Combinations are putting two or more things together. In math we talk about how many *different* combinations there
are of specific items. They also saw a small table with two columns,
FOOD and DRINK, and several options (Pizza, Salad, Tacos, Water,
Milk) underneath each title.

"If I were trying to pick out a lunch," Lebowitz announced, "and I
could only pick one food item and one drink, how many combinations
could I make?"

Harvey shifted in his chair, while two of the students at his cluster of desks raised their hands. Ms. Schmidt stirred her tea, staring
straight ahead. It was her turn to be tired.

◇ ◇ ◇ **B** ◇ ◇ ◇

Zakiya Reid watched the nine parents crowd into her tiny office and realized that she'd been tricked. She hadn't expected to see Fred there—they'd clashed before—but there he was. And then he handed her the report.

It felt like an intimidation campaign, but as she listened to Fred's summary of the report, she was surprised to hear the suggestion that *she* was the one doing the intimidating. "There is widespread fear among the Bancroft faculty that you will retaliate against those who dare to speak out or disagree with you," Fred reported.

Seriously? Reid thought to herself. People feel *abused*? Seriously? It's not like I get a lot of forewarning from DCPS when new initiatives come up. It's not like I can give people a serious heads-up—I don't even know what's coming myself most of the time.

As she looked at the half-moon of angry parents before her, Zakiya Reid felt the fatigue from trying to negotiate all these relationships and ways of doing things. "You don't realize how it will impact your psyche," she told me later. "So I told the parents that I agreed teacher voice needed to be strengthened—and that I could do a better job with that. I think the confusion has come from the fact that Bancroft has historically operated in its own world. They decided to do foreign language on their own, they decided to do full inclusion on their own, and these were decisions that were possible at that time. But now DCPS is trying to get out in front of all these issues."

Even before the meeting, Zakiya had known morale was low. At department team meetings, people were actively questioning the school's heightened attention to data. And her decision to institute new report card guidelines had ruffled some feathers. "We're trying to standardize across the school so parents can get information that's as accurate as possible," she explained. "You can't just go around giving kids 4s because you feel like it—you have to start talking *really* about where kids are at."

As she packed up to head home for the evening, Zakiya grabbed a copy of Fred's report, and an early projection of her budget for next year. The school's commitment to having two teachers in every classroom was in serious jeopardy, a result of the changing demographics in the neighborhood and the reduction of low-income families in the early grades.

A week earlier, Ms. Reid's supervisor had urged her to get her kids to 50% proficiency in reading by year's end. "Are you kidding?" she said. "We're at 38% and many of our teachers can't teach."

"Do you know where you are?" the supervisor replied. "There's a plan for Bancroft—there are million-dollar homes around here. You have people who could choose your school right now if they wanted to. It's time for you to reel them in."

## CHAPTER NINE

# Playing the Game

◇ ◇ ◇ **MV** ◇ ◇ ◇

"THAT DOESN'T LOOK LIKE an airplane—it looks like a jet!"
"Hey, this is the way to my house!"
"14th Street! 14th Street has a bridge to Virginnnia."
"Look down right there! It looks like clown cars."

It's late April, and the kindergartners of Mundo Verde are aboard a black bus, traveling out of the city toward Romey Pittman's farm. The inside smells strongly of diesel fuel, and most of the children are wearing jackets they no longer need. In the front of the bus, alongside their teachers, boxes overflow with the students' tools of the day: butterfly nets, jars, clipboards, juice boxes, and apples.

The bus turns left off Florida Avenue and onto Route 50.

"I've never been on a highway when there's a school day."
"Look guys! We're in the asteroid place. Look out for asteroids!"
"McDonald's!"

Forty minutes later, the bus passes into Anne Arundel County in Maryland. It's quieter inside, but voices of children still fill the air.

"I think we're in the countryside. Look at all those trees."
"Whoa—this is a long way from school."
"We're running out of gas, right?"

The driver pulls off on a private lane, and the sounds of passing cars fade in favor of the slow churn of gravel underneath the bus's large tires. Soon the students will begin their "field work"—a phrase schools in the Expeditionary Learning network use intentionally. "We call this field work because it's not a trip or a tour," Romey explains, "as much as it is a chance to gather information and behave like scientists. It's active, not passive."

For the previous six weeks, Molly and Berenice had been steadily working on the students' BBK—an acronym for Building Background Knowledge—to make sure their time in the field was well spent. In Spanish, the students studied everything there was to know about Monarch butterflies, from what they eat (milkweed) to how they manage to travel such long distances and arrive each year in the same place at the same time. And in English, they researched different animals and the origins of their particular adaptations.

Today is the first time the students will directly confront the subjects of their study. They will catch—and then try to draw to scale—a butterfly. They will catch—and then observe, back in Molly's room—tadpoles. And they will search for actual milkweed plants, and bring them back to feed the hungry caterpillars in Berenice's room.

Once the bus is unloaded, everyone gathers in front of Romey's house. Hens strut fearlessly nearby, while solar panels on the roof reflect the morning's ample sun. Most of the children run off their energy by chasing one another in wide, concentric circles.

After a while the students are broken into groups and head off toward different stations. At one, they play an outdoor variation of hide-and-seek called The Hawk and the Mouse. At another, they scan the pond for tadpoles and algae, scooping both into large mason jars. The group with Romey—whose family has inhabited this land since the early 18th century—learns about local plants and habitats.

"This is a paw paw plant," she instructs. "And that is a Jack-in-the-pulpit." The boys in the group half-listen, and half-scan the ground for sticks. Off in the distance, Molly hikes with purpose between stations, determined to keep each train running on time.

In a large meadow, another group searches for butterflies. The children wave colorful nets high above their heads. A few actually catch one; the rest run joyfully in nonlinear pursuit. I walk with Molly as she leaves to check another station. "Part of today is just giving everyone a chance to be outside and play. This is what every five-year-old should do *every day*. It's less about the discrete outcome. I think running in a butterfly field is its own outcome. We talk about sustainability a lot at our school, but part of developing a real commitment to environmentalism comes from just being outside. And a lot of these kids don't get regular opportunities to do that."

Molly catches up to the group at the pond, where she comes upon Stephen and Elan, walking slightly behind the group. "Elan, if you want I can carry your backpack," Stephen says. "Would you like that?"

"He swears he's in love with school now," Molly tells me. "I'm pretty hard on him because I have such high expectations. He's really bright, and I think he's been bored a lot of the time. But he's really engaged in the expedition; he loves learning about frogs."

Molly felt more engaged, too. "I absolutely love the focus on learning targets," she says. "In the fall, we didn't really use them. But now I always explicitly state what our target is, and the kids are using the same language when they talk to me; they're internalizing it and seeing the purpose of what we're doing. That's what we want—it's not just about doing the work, it's seeing the purpose. And they can see the exact way they make progress. They're able to see themselves grow.

"I'm excited about the new expedition," she continues, "because I can see all of its different stages and how they fit together. I go home most nights and talk about adaptations with my friends. And because of that I feel more able to brush off the rough spots of the school. I have fewer bad days now."

While Molly and I speak, Stephen tries to draw a salamander. For weeks, he has been studying the use of camouflage as an adaptation. Like the other children, he has already completed five drafts of his scientific drawing. And like the rest, he has clearly seen his own improvement, and grown in confidence as a result.

"We still need to outline each drawing so it pops before we can take it to the publisher," Molly says, "and their explanatory text needs one more round of revision. It's been a real push to get them to focus on the 'why'—why does this adaptation matter? Why is it important? I think it's just developmentally hard. But we're trying to get them to see they're not just writing for themselves—they're writing for people that know nothing about adaptation. I want this book to be beautiful, and to show them just how good their work can be. That's why the public presentation part of the expedition is so important."

◊   ◊   ◊   **B**   ◊   ◊   ◊

On the playground behind their school, the students of room 121 run off their lunch before a final afternoon of preparation for next week's DC-CAS exam. Almost every student has fallen into a predictable gender role. The boys sprint and scream at each other on the soccer pitch, while in the shade nearby the girls play cards or a game of "family."

Two students go against type; Ernesto, who always prefers the quiet energy of the girls to the chaotic contests of the boys; and Lourdes, who dominates the athletic action with a ferocity and skill that belies her slight frame. She barks instructions at her teammates, her low-slung ponytail drenched in sweat.

Nearby, Ms. Lebowitz sits and half-observes the game before her. Mya, legs thin as toothpicks, sits next to her. At the beginning of the year, Mya was one of the lowest-scoring readers; now, on the eve of the DC-CAS, she has become the class's biggest success story. "I'm nervous because I heard it's going to be really hard and it takes like five days," she confessed. Ms. Lebowitz stroked her hair and smiled. "You're ready for this," she told her. "Just do your best and don't worry about anything else."

Mya skipped off, and I asked Lebowitz what it felt like to teach third grade in a system that placed such high stakes on a single test. "I feel more relaxed this year," she said. "Last year was a much more pervasive sense of test prep at the school; the kids from the lower grades came into our classroom and did cheers. But this year there was nothing.

"I think the emphasis we place on this test is out of proportion," she continued, while the students began lining up to head back in and upstairs. "But I also think as long as the teachers aren't overly nervous, the kids won't be, either. We're playing the game so they can be players in the game."

An hour later, Bancroft's third-graders cycle through math stations to do some final tune-ups before the test. On their desks are collages of worksheets in both reading and math: *Which of the following is a good*

*example of the fact that 10 divided by 2 equals 5? Which of the following is a good supporting detail from paragraph 2?*

In preparation for exam week, anything on the walls that could help students recall things they should have memorized has been removed. The corner that housed "Our Best Work" is now bare white cinderblock. Big pieces of blue paper have been hung over the Word Wall. Only the emoticon plates remain.

Rebecca Lebowitz works with one group on area and perimeter. The children have notecards and are writing answers down and silently handing them to their teacher for confirmation. Rebecca Schmidt works with a different group on the same subject, and speaks quietly to me about what's happening in her room. "Area and perimeter *are* developmentally appropriate concepts—they can access this information cognitively," she begins. "But the way it's presented to us and tested by the state just isn't very interesting. With reading and writing, it's easier to make things relevant. It's much harder in math. Plus, we have so many standards here we need to cover. I've heard it's a lot thinner in other countries."

The groups rotate, and a new cluster of children comes to work on reasoning skills with Ms. Schmidt. "We want them to do more reasoning," she says, "but the reasoning tends to get lost amidst the 'tricks' they need to get the answers right. The urgency of the test makes it hard to get to the bigger, deeper ideas. And because they're assessed that way, we end up teaching that way."

Later, after the students have all gone home, Ms. Schmidt slips into a different room and changes into a different set of clothes. Today is her final-round interview for a fellowship at the U.S. Department of Education—a year-long appointment in which just five classroom teachers from across the country get embedded in different departments at the DOE, the idea being that their on-the-ground experience can help shape and inform the policy decisions being made by federal officials. Ms. Schmidt takes out a pair of black dress shoes from her backpack and tries to calm her nerves.

"I think it will help me that I'm coming from DCPS, because we're at the forefront of reform right now," she tells me just before leaving the school. "That's why I applied to teach in D.C. the first place. But what strikes me is we've made so many changes in how teachers are paid and assessed, yet teachers are still leaving the district in large numbers. My HR records are no longer being lost in some folder somewhere, but something's still broken. What do teachers really need in order to stay?"

As Kristin Scotchmer and Dahlia Aguilar reviewed the thick document in front of them—an implementation review instrument from Expeditionary Learning, designed to help schools gauge the extent to which they instituted high-quality EL practices—they started to realize their plans to coordinate Mundo Verde's many different review processes would not be possible. Later in the day, they had a meeting with a representative from the Office of the State Superintendent of Education (OSSE)—the organization that sets policies and ensures accountability for all public education in D.C. Early next week, they were set to meet with their chief liaison from the Public Charter School Board (PCSB), the organization that has the power to grant (and revoke) their charter.

Because each organization has its own year-end reporting documents, Kristin had hoped to create some efficiencies in their completion of all three. But as she and Dahlia reviewed the specificity of the EL review, it became clear there were no efficiencies to be had. "Our teachers haven't been steeped all year in the language EL uses," said Dahlia. "That makes our affiliation with them both easier and harder. There's a blueprint in place for us to follow, and yet the existence of the blueprint lays bare some of our operational challenges as a year-one school."

"This is going to take a long time to unpack in Spanish," Kristin added. "Let's revisit this after the OSSE meeting." She packed up a few other documents in front of her and headed to the conference room, where an OSSE representative was waiting for her.

The night before, she'd learned that the school's application to move into the J. F. Cook School—along with, curiously, every other application for the space—had been denied. Kristin already knew that finding buildings was one of the central challenges of a charter school leader—despite the surplus of abandoned schools in the city. At the same time, the Cook school had seemed so perfect, and their application had felt so strong. Now her search for a long-term home would have to be suspended in place of finding a one- or two-year bridge location. And the clock was ticking; Mundo Verde would be homeless beginning July 1.

"I want to make sure everything is aligned with your funding and check your 'burn rate,'" the OSSE representative said as he handed her another thick booklet, this one OSSE's monitoring handbook. Kristin thumbed through hundreds of pages of rubrics and reporting criteria. "But first," he continued, "why don't you start off by tooting your own horn a little bit. After all, we haven't been here since September."

While Kristin met with OSSE, Dahlia dipped into the kindergarten classrooms to see how the expeditions were taking shape. On the English side, the Lions were working on revising the drafts of the descriptions they had written for their scientific drawings. Dahlia knelt down next to Freya to see what she had written.

*Draft 3:* the Grate Hornd OWL has clos so it can grab on to Branchis and Cech ther FOOD. The Owl Flis rily Fast so thea Hav to grab on.

*Draft 4:* _____

_____

_____.

Molly walked around the room to check in with different students. On her desk, in front of the fish tank where the tadpoles had almost all become full-fledged frogs, was a stack of children's drawings. Each set of drafts was held together by a paper clip, along with the original photo. The backs of the drawings were where Molly delivered her feedback, which was always couched in encouraging terms. "I notice your legs look like rectangles," she wrote on one child's early draft. "Would you consider making them curve a bit?"

After 15 minutes or so, the class's attention started to ebb; the boys began using their pencils as spaceships. Molly sensed the change and shifted the activity; the early finishers moved to the carpet for independent reading.

Freya stayed at her table, absorbed in reviewing—and perfecting—her draft. She pointed her pencil at each word, reading out loud to herself and seeing if it sounded right.

"I'm really impressed you took the time to correct all of your capital letters," Molly told her after reading her latest draft.

> The grate hornd owl has clos so it can grab on to branches and cech ther food. The owl flis rilly fast so they hav to grab on to the branch.

Dahlia got up to head to the Spanish room. Several large pieces of construction paper were spread out across the floor as she entered, at which different students were at different stages of drawing out butterfly wings big enough to turn five-year-olds into Monarchs. Berenice stood at the edge of the green rug, speaking rapidly and with great animation while a semicircle of students huddled around her. They were practicing their lines for the film the class was making about Monarchs, and Berenice was demonstrating how to inject the right amount of emotion and affect into each line.

Nearby, Stephen worked one-on-one with a parent volunteer. Behind them, butcher paper on the wall mapped out the seven set designs the film would require. Just two weeks remained until the whole community—parents, siblings, board members—would come together to see what the children had done.

When it comes to transforming American public education, nothing matters more than determining how students—and, now, teachers—are assessed. And when it comes to understanding the possibilities and pitfalls of assessment itself, no one knows more than Harvard's Daniel Koretz.

For years, Koretz has been researching the effects of high-stakes testing programs on how teachers teach—and students learn. In 2008, he published the book *Measuring Up: What Educational Testing Really Tells Us*, to share his insights. "Careful testing can give us tremendously valuable information about student achievement that we would otherwise lack," he says. The question is how well we understand what standardized tests can, and cannot, tell us about American schools. "There is no optimal design," he asserts. "Rather, designing a testing program is an exercise in trade-offs and compromise—and a judgment about which compromise is best."

Although modern conversations about testing point to the passage of No Child Left Behind as our country's watershed moment, the history of testing in America goes back much further than that—all the way back to the 1840s, in fact. But Koretz believes the modern chapter of testing begins more recently—not in 2002, but during the 1950s, when few states required testing programs but many districts administered their own; when the tests themselves were largely or entirely multiple choice; and when the results were primarily used to help teachers identify the relative strengths and weaknesses of their students. "These tests were not treated as trivial," Koretz explains, "but in most instances students and teachers did not stand to suffer any dire consequences or reap any rewards as a result of the scores."[1]

This began to change in the 1960s, thanks to two actions by the federal government: the 1965 passage of the Elementary and Secondary Education Act (ESEA), which deepened the federal government's involvement in American public education and established a program, Title I, that provided extra funds to low-income schools like Bancroft; and the 1969 debut of the National Assessment of Educational Progress (NAEP), an annual sampling of American students that has come to be known as The Nation's Report Card. "In retrospect it seems that these two federal programs marked the onset of a sea change in educational testing in the United States," Koretz explains. "They signified the beginning of a fundamental shift in the goals of testing, from diagnosis and local evaluation to large-scale monitoring of performance and, ultimately, to test-based accountability."[2]

By the end of the 1970s, 35 states had set up their own testing programs—mostly exit exams students had to pass in order to graduate. According to Koretz, this was the final stage of the mental shift. "The idea behind traditional achievement tests was that standardized tests should improve instruction by providing educators and parents with useful information they would otherwise lack." The new idea posited a very different proposition: "that instruction could be improved by holding someone—in this case, students, but it could also be educators—directly accountable for performance on tests."[3]

By the time educators like Rebecca Schmidt and Rebecca Lebowitz began their careers in the D.C. public schools, the idea of accountability had extended to teacher accountability as well. On that point, scholars like Koretz are unequivocal. "It is inappropriate to use a score from a single test, without additional information, to assign students to special education, to hold students back, to screen students for first-time enrollment, to evaluate the effectiveness of an entire educational system, or to identify the 'best' teachers or schools."

"Critics who ignore the impact of social factors on test scores miss the point," Koretz argues. "The reason to acknowledge their influence is not to let anyone off the hook but to get the right answer. Certainly, low scores are a sign that something is amiss. . . . But the low scores themselves don't tell *why* achievement is low and are usually insufficient to tell us where instruction is good or bad, just as a fever by itself is insufficient to reveal what illness a child has. Disappointing scores can mask good instruction, and high scores can hide problems that need to be addressed."[4]

Back in 1951, the University of Iowa's E. F. Lindquist argued for similar caution. Like Koretz, Lindquist was a researcher on core issues of educational assessment; unlike Koretz, he was arguably the person most responsible for fostering the development and use of standardized tests in the United States, having helped design not just several of Iowa's state assessments, but also the ACT, GED, and National Merit Scholarship test. He even had a hand in the invention of the first optical scanner for scoring tests—an innovation with cotton gin-like implications for the exponential spread of standardized testing in the decades that followed.

Lindquist was, in other words, about as far from "anti-testing" as you could be. Yet he also understood a fundamental principle about assessment, and about teaching and learning itself. "The only perfectly valid measure of the attainment of an educational objective," he wrote, "would be one based on direct observation of the natural behavior of individuals."

◇  ◇  ◇  **B**  ◇  ◇  ◇

On the morning of the first day of test week, Lourdes feeds pencil after pencil into the electric sharpener on her teachers' desk. Twenty-two of her classmates are spread across the desks of room 121, where each uses a three-flapped manila folder as a makeshift wall to block wandering eyes.

While Lourdes sharpens and Ms. Lebowitz waits to gather the five Special Education students who will be tested in a separate room upstairs, the other children eat their state-provided breakfasts and chat about the days ahead.

"I should have guessed they'd give us Cinnamon Toast Crunch on the first day of the DC-CAS," says Elliott, his hair a bird's nest mapping the previous night's tosses and turns. "Every other day they give us Kix."

"I'm scared," Mya confesses.

"I'm not scared," Lourdes adds. "I studied and I got a good night's sleep."

The loudspeaker interrupts their conversation.

"Are you all ready for this?" Ms. Reid urges. "Today is the DC-CAS. Do your best, check your work, and you're all going to do awesome!"

Harvey arrives as the rest of the students are finishing their breakfasts. He walks up sheepishly to Ms. Lebowitz, thumbs in his pockets. She smiles down at him.

"You ready for today?"

"No."

"Let's try to get in the zone," Lebowitz implores. "What does it look and sound like?"

Harvey sways quietly, and Lourdes chimes in. "It's real quiet like there's no one here."

"Why is it important to be quiet during the test?" Ms. Schmidt adds.

"Because noise can be really distracting," says Ernesto.

"Can anyone think of a time they were really focused?" Ms. Lebowitz asks the room.

"Think about what helps you stay focused, and try to feel that way today. This test is in the bag. It's a measure of how much we've taught you—not how smart you are. So don't worry if you come across something you don't know—and try your best."

At 9:15 A.M., Ms. Schmidt heads downstairs to pick up the tests in the school counseling office. A long line of classroom teachers extends out into the hallway. After several minutes, she collects her materials— a black plastic briefcase; a Ziploc bag of even more pencils; and a box of Kleenex. She signs the materials sheet before she leaves: SCHMIDT 121.

When she returns, Lourdes greets her expectantly. "Are those the tests?" she asks. "Is it heavy?"

At 9:30 A.M., Ms. Reid addresses the school over the loudspeaker a final time. "You're ready!" she yells. "Now it's time to blast the DC-CAS!"

Two hours later, most of the students have finished. They sit at their desks, legs and feet rocking, heads resting in hands, reading their own books in silent obedience. A few of the children are still working, including Lourdes, whose morning confidence has retreated in the face of the actual exam. Ms. Schmidt makes eye contact with her, nodding positively. Lourdes shakes her head discouragingly in response.

Up to that point, in the quiet of the morning, Schmidt has been reviewing her final interview for the DOE fellowship in her mind. There had been 12 of them, seated at a roundtable in the middle of a room, and more than 40 DOE staff surrounding them in silent observation. She knew one of the other candidates personally—a fellow teacher who was five years older, but whose career path and interests mirrored Rebecca's own—and was surprised to feel an almost primal competitiveness rise up inside her.

Their first assignment was to debate a policy proposal about teacher training and then come up with some talking points that would help U.S. education secretary Arne Duncan convince colleges of education across the country to support the idea. "The others all started off on the wrong wavelength," Schmidt recalled, "whereas my nemesis and I got straight to the speech, and what needed to be said. I kept hammering away at the importance of messaging, and what I'd learned about it—good and bad—from my experiences in D.C."

By the time she got home that night, Schmidt was already half-asleep, her voice deep and croaky from all the interviews and the public projections of confidence. "They told me I should hear in a week or so," she said as the first day of test week drew to a close. "But I feel like I did what I had to do. We'll see."

◇  ◇  ◇  **MV**  ◇  ◇  ◇

By the time Karen Copeland received the postcard in the mail saying her daughter had won a preschool seat at one of D.C.'s newest charter schools, she had just about given up hope. Every other school had drawn Lia's name so far after the cut off as to become comic. She hadn't even attended an open house for the school whose offer of admission she now held in her hand. But as she thumbed through her folder of handouts from the Charter School expo, she started to remember being impressed by the school—Creative Minds International—and by its charismatic founding principal.

She found the school's glossy handout. *Opening Fall 2012*, it read, alongside the color images of two children's faces:

> *NEW International Public Charter School with Arts, Foreign Languages and hands-on, Project-Based Learning. Creative Minds International Public Charter School is a new, tuition-free school for children in Washington, DC. Creative Minds International offers an engaging, diverse, international curriculum with project- and arts-based activities that foster creativity, self-motivation, social and emotional development as well as academic excellence.*

How can a school say it "offers" something, she thought, if it doesn't even exist? Then she read more about the school—iMacs in every classroom, an emphasis on the arts, and a founding principal with a PhD and a deep understanding of how children learn—and in spite of herself, Karen Copeland started to feel the fortune of her winning number.

She also had no other options—a fact that tempered her enthusiasm when she attended a special open house for admitted families the following week. "This is the actual reality of school choice," she told me as we entered the school's facilities to pick up Lia's enrollment pack for the 2012–2013 school year. "It's school *chance*. The most established charter schools have basically stopped being anything other than a true lottery ticket for families, because most of the spots for the younger grades are taken by siblings. That means for those of us who still want to play the game, the best options are the unproven schools—the ones that sound great on paper, and that may actually *become* great, but which don't yet exist in any real form. You're buying low and hoping the stock will jump."

As Karen walked in the school's first-year front doors, just off a busy stretch of 16th Street in Columbia Heights, she saw other families coming in to submit their enrollment materials. The foyer still featured the mottos and posters of the building's current tenant—a charter high school that was about to move across town. One set of parents brought their son with them. "I don't like it," he said moments after entering, at which point his father knelt down beside him. "This isn't the school yet," he said. The boy stared back blankly. "What is it then?"

Nearby, another parent handed over her daughter's materials and gave the young female teacher on the other side of the table a bear hug. "If you all need help getting ready for the fall, let me know."

"That gives me goosebumps," the teacher responded. "I think I might cry."

Karen moved through the entryway and into a large room where Creative Minds' principal was addressing prospective families. "I'm wondering how much balance you'll be able to maintain once the school year actually starts," Karen said, arms crossed. "Lia's got 17+ years of schooling ahead of her. I don't want her to get pushed too quickly into an academic focus."

"I know exactly what you mean," the principal responded. "I started this school out of the same frustrations I'd felt when I was searching for a school for my son several years ago. That's why we want to make sure our teachers are just as focused on addressing the social and emotional needs of your children as they are on their academics."

Karen watched the other parents around her nod in affirmation at what they heard. Are these future friends? Will Lia be spending time at these people's homes? Should I believe what this principal is telling me?

We left shortly thereafter. Karen thumbed through the enrollment package outside the school's front doors. Request for Records. Race and Ethnicity Data Collection. Home Language Survey. Emergency Contact Information. Residency Verification.

"I get excited every time I learn more about the school," Karen said. "But at the same time, did you see how young those teachers were in there? I worry that what's happening is that the rising expectations of the parents and the increased understanding of the research has outstripped the capacity of the teachers to actually deliver the goods. Some of what I heard in there sounded like an election speech; it all sounds so good in theory. What will it look like in practice? And do I want Lia to be a part of the experiment?

"The more I think about it," Karen continued as new arrivals brushed past her, "I'm not as concerned that they're a new school. It's *preschool*. By the time she gets to first grade, they'll have worked out the kinks. I go back and forth on where my priorities are. On one level I say let's try this and I'm OK with her switching schools a few times. But I also can't help but think about the tumult down the line.

"It's a leap of faith—but I suppose that's true anywhere." She unlocked her car to drive back home, two miles to the east. "I think we'll still move out of the city," she mused, "just not right away."

On the final day of test week, Rebecca Lebowitz hurries the group through a modified morning meeting, all prior doubts of the activity's value having long since disappeared. "Yesterday I buy a shirt and a pants," says a student whose family left Honduras just a few years prior. "I'm ready for questions."

While the class inquires further—"What color were they? How much did they cost?"—Rebecca Schmidt returns with the familiar black plastic briefcase, and, because it's the last day, a cardboard box filled with bags of Cheetos. "It's been getting easier each day," she tells me on the way back to the room, "because the kids know the drill. At the same time, they're also getting more fatigued, so they're starting to just fill in the sheets. It hasn't been a terrible experience for anyone, but I feel like only about half of this is useful to me or the system."

Three hours later, all of the students have finished. "If you can hear my voice, put your hands on your head," Ms. Schmidt whispers as she walks between their desks. Her students smile in response and do as they're told. "If you can hear my voice, wave your hands in the air. I want to congratulate you for finishing the DC-CAS," she says happily. "And to celebrate such awesome reading and thinking and calculating, we're going to do some relaxing the rest of the way."

As Ms. Schmidt speaks, Ms. Lebowitz sets up the projector at the foot of the rug and presses play. The students shout in excitement and grab bags of Cheetos as they crowd on the rug. The Spanish version of the animated film *Rio* begins, and multicolored birds of every variety sing the movie's opening number. A few of the children sing along in Spanish.

An hour later, most of them are still watching. Some have begun to flirt furtively—hand on hand, head in lap—while others have fallen asleep. Ms. Schmidt snaps the clasp of the black briefcase and heads downstairs to hand in the exams.

In four months, the results will be in.

## CHAPTER TEN

# Vuela, Vuela Mariposa!

◊  ◊  ◊  **B**  ◊  ◊  ◊

WHILE THE LONG ROW of eight-year-olds in front of him crouched behind a low-slung wall, Harvey straddled the top of the second-story jungle gym that overlooked the back of his school, surrounded by his fellow third-graders.

"Wait for the music, everyone!" Ms. Schmidt shouted. "Here it comes!"

The song they'd learned by heart crackled out over what looked like a set of World War II-era loudspeakers.

*Give me freedom*
*Give me fire*
*Give me reasons*
*Take me higher*

As Harvey peered down from his perch, he felt like he could see the entire school below him. The kindergartners stood in a circle on the soccer field, holding the edges of a colorful parachute. The fifth-graders lined opposite sides of the field just beyond them, angling giant flags out to form a canopy the cameraman would soon pass through—the final act of a music video that would be filmed in a single shot, pass through every hallway, and feature every student and employee of the school.

Harvey heard muffled singing inside. They were close.

*See the champions*
*Take the field now*
*You define us*
*Make us feel proud*

The door opened and the cameraman emerged. The second-graders popped out from behind the wall, while Harvey and the other students around the jungle gym held up homemade signs.

*Nosotros ♥ Bancroft!*
*Leyendo al novel del grado.*
*Bancroft Rocks!*

The cameraman moved past and began to descend the long stairway that led to the main playground behind the school. Students scurried to the edge of the landing to watch the rest of the show. Some kindergartners performed the Macarena on the stairwell; others made the parachute rise and fall. The flags of the fifth-graders swayed back and forth as the song neared its final stanza.

*When I get older*
*When I get older*
*I will be stronger*
*Just like a wavin' flag*

"That looked great," the cameraman said as the song ended, and the children cheered. "I think we're ready."

◊ ◊ ◊ MV ◊ ◊ ◊

Berenice Pernalete scanned her surroundings a final time; everything appeared to be in order. Over the past 10 weeks, her room had become its own mini-forest: billowy trees made out of brown and green tissue paper, oversized orange and black butterfly wings, and neatly framed pictures documenting the stages of a Monarch's metamorphosis: small drawings of their bodies; medium diagrams of their life cycle; and large paintings of their habitat. Berenice searched through a pile of colorful children's drawings on her desk. "We're missing a really important document," she said to no one in particular. "Here it is." She pasted the document to the wall, straightened her oversized brown belt and removed a piece of glitter from her black dress. Ready to go.

Outside, Mundo Verde's other teachers were finishing final preparations of their own. While Kristin Scotchmer interviewed a prospective new teacher in the conference room—the school was about to double in size, and the sooner their new colleagues were in place, the sooner they could all plan together for Year Two—Dahlia Aguilar sat with a four-year-old who'd been brought to her office after punching another child. "Sometimes you can seek a conflict, even if a person doesn't seek you out," she counseled.

The front door of the school opened, and Molly Howard entered with a large cardboard box. "I need scissors!" she cried.

The other teachers stopped what they were doing to watch Molly tear open the box. She pulled out a book and read the title out loud: *Why Do Animals Look the Way They Look?*

"It's beautiful!" said one teacher.

"Look at all that color!" said another.

Molly admired the cover and the drawings inside. Then she remembered the last bit of work to be done on the documentation panel in her classroom. "How much time do we have left?" she asked.

"Forty-five minutes."

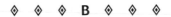

Zakiya Reid called the final staff meeting of the year to order with a rhythmic clap, her due-any-day belly bulging underneath her purple dress. "I want us to give ourselves a round of applause," she began. "We're the only school in DCPS to win the TEAM award two years in a row."

"What's the TEAM award?" one teacher asked.

"It's a way to recognize schools like ours that have showed real gains in our scores. But what I haven't told you yet is that every teacher in the school will also receive a cash reward."

The room broke out in applause. "I'm not sure when the money will arrive exactly," she added, "but it should be here before October.

And we still need to put together a final package of materials to submit to the organization that sponsors the award."

"Should I be saving some of the children's work?" asked a kindergarten teacher. "I've just started sending it all home."

"The artifacts they're interested in don't involve student work," Reid replied. "It's more like templates and strategies for improving our math scores.

"Meanwhile—this just in. I attended the leadership academy last week and central office says they want us to be having more fun. Of course they also said we need to make sure instruction keeps happening through the last day of school next week. So let's just do what we can to give the year a fun conclusion and also go hard until the end. Summer is right around the corner."

◇  ◇  ◇  **MV**  ◇  ◇  ◇

As Dahlia Aguilar wrote down a few words to share before her school community crowded into the *Zocalo* for the culminating event of the year, she allowed the unresolved anxieties that had been consuming her to ebb. Although Kristin had finally found a new, albeit temporary, home—a building just off 16th Street in Columbia Heights they would share with a brand-new school—they wouldn't be able to start moving in until a month before the year was going to start. Although Mundo Verde had already exploded in popularity—their waiting list for Year Two stretched well into the 400s—there was no way to guarantee that new families would maintain a healthy mix between English and Spanish speakers. There were those three different final reports that had to be filed. They needed to raise more money. They had to hire new staff. And all of these things needed to be resolved as quickly as possible.

Tonight, though, was about celebrating the work that had been completed thus far. Five-year-olds publishing a book of scientific drawings about animal adaptations, *and* producing a film about the migratory pattern of the Monarch butterfly? Amazing. Dahlia watched a few parent volunteers arranging the chairs. Her own high school was full of kids like theirs. "We were a school of poor Brown and Black kids that no one outside of our community expected very much from," she said. "But our teachers and families expected the world of us."

Dahlia finished her notes and stood at the school's front door. The parents had started arriving, and she planned to welcome every one.

◊　◊　◊　**B**　◊　◊　◊

Rebecca Lebowitz led her class into the gymnasium, trying to calm the nerves of the day's few performers. Elliott walked next to her, twirling his tinfoil-covered hat and sword. "Remember to pace yourself," she told him. "And have fun."

The stage was framed by a giant hand-painted sign, RECITAL DE POESIA, in front of which was a small judge's table and three plastic yellow chairs. Most of the school had already arrived. The intensity of test week behind them, Bancroft's final weeks had been marked by a steady series of community-oriented events: the poetry recital, the science fair, an evening writing celebration, the all-school video. The students huddled closely together on the ground, while a small group of parents behind them scattered across four rows of brown metal folding chairs.

"¡Bienvenidos, Bancroft!" a teacher shouted from the stage. "Today is a celebration of our school's two languages, and a chance to see how well you can speak and write in Spanish."

"Are you getting stage fright?" Ernesto whispered to Lourdes, who had a faraway look in her eyes. "Breathe," Ms. Schmidt told her.

As the program began, the first performer didn't do anything to help calm the nerves of the others. She brought her teacher up with her, afraid she'd forget her lines. When she did, her cheeks quickly lined with tears. She exited the stage as soon as her poem was completed and ran into the arms of her father, who wiped her cheeks and whispered encouragingly to her.

Elliott was next, reciting a passage from *Don Quixote*. He delivered his lines flawlessly and with flair. His mom beamed her approval from the first row of chairs, while his little brother watched intently.

Lourdes was one of the final performers to go. She recited stiffly—she was an athlete, after all, not an actor—her body dwarfed by the size of the stage on which she stood. But when she finished and the applause started, she paused at center stage for an extended beat, arms on her head, reluctant to leave.

The recital ended, and Ms. Lebowitz led the class back upstairs for a brief break. Later that afternoon, they'd do the final filming of *Bancroft Pride*. Lourdes walked alongside her teacher, keeping the program open to the page with her name. "Look, Missus," she said. "This is meeee."

◊  ◊  ◊  **MV**  ◊  ◊  ◊

Ten minutes before show time, the seats in the *Zocalo* were all filled. Berenice and Dahlia were alone in Berenice's classroom, going over final logistics.

"How long should we keep each group?" Dahlia asked.

"Let's say about 10 minutes," Berenice replied. "And then you can come and tell them to switch."

Dahlia took another look around the room. "Your classroom looks really beautiful," she said. "Do you want to say anything before we start?"

"Definitely not," Berenice said.

"OK. See you out there in a second."

Dahlia opened the door, and the swirling din of young and old voices leaked in. When it closed behind her, Berenice was alone with the silent rhythmic hum of the A/C. "These kids are about to have the greatest night of their lives," she said.

"*¡Buenos noches a todos y bienvenidos a Mundo Verde!*" Dahlia began, as more and more bodies squeezed into the tiny space, which had become hot enough to prompt the parents of young children to strip them down to their diapers. Romey craned her neck from the back to see.

The Lions and Zebras had no such problem; they were all bunched together on the ground, just inches from the screen and Dahlia's feet as she spoke; the room smelled like stale sweat. "What an exciting night! We have friends and family and some really exciting learning to share with you. Expeditions are journeys you take that involve a little bit of risk and a little bit of danger. Tonight you'll get to see what your children produced during that expedition, and a little later, you'll get to go into their classrooms and go on the same journey they did. But for now, I present you the world premiere of *Vuela, Vuela Mariposa!*"

◇  ◇  ◇  **B**  ◇  ◇  ◇

While her students took their places on or around the jungle gym for the video's final take, Rebecca Schmidt tried to summon the same level of excitement she saw in their faces. By involving every grade and every classroom, the video project had injected the school with a heightened sense of community. The day before, however, Ms. Schmidt learned that the Department of Education had chosen five other teachers for the fellowship—including her nemesis. At this point, her only option was a new charter school that had been recruiting her. She loved the idea of the place—a demonstration school that would train teachers and actively model great teaching—and she had felt a real connection with the school's articulate, twenty-something principal. But they hadn't even been able to tell her what they'd pay her—they couldn't know until they saw their final enrollment numbers the following fall—and when she'd spoken to one of their teachers, he said something that excited and terrified her in equal measure. "Everything you're afraid of is exactly what's happening," he said. "And I wouldn't trade it for anything."

Maybe I just need a change in attitude, she thought to herself as she massaged the soreness out of her calves; the D.C. Marathon had been the previous weekend. Maybe I just need to decide on something and stick to it. Maybe I'll feel rejuvenated in a new school.

"OK everyone," she yelled. "Here it comes!"

◇  ◇  ◇  **MV**  ◇  ◇  ◇

As soon as the first faces appeared on the screen in the darkened room, the kindergartners of Mundo Verde erupted in sound.

*There are too many butterflies here, we need to leave.*
*It is getting colder and colder.*

Albert held up his leg to his chin. Jimmy watched himself deliver a line and squeezed the leg of the nearest adult. The children's mouths were hanging open, their eyes wide, rapt.

*Welcome, Monarch Butterflies!*
*We will protect you.*
*We plant trees all year long.*

The rise and fall of their screams overwhelmed the audio of their film. More than screams even, the sounds they were making were guttural, theatrical, unprecedented surges of a thrill they didn't think was possible. Berenice was right: it was the greatest night of their lives—so much so that as soon as the movie ended, and they saw themselves bowing to their imaginary audience on screen, the *Zocalo* filled with the spontaneous, steady chants of the children:

"Again! Again! AGAIN!"

◇ ◇ ◇ **B** ◇ ◇ ◇

On the last Monday of the school year, Ms. Schmidt and Ms. Lebowitz told the children they would not be coming back. It was the day of the class's writing celebration, so while they prepared to deliver the news, their students' parents filled the hallway outside their classroom, setting up the different potluck dishes that would accompany a day of listening to each other's stories.

"This morning, we decided we'd read you our favorite book," Ms. Lebowitz announced, as Ms. Schmidt sat next to her. "It's called *Oh the Places You'll Go!* by Dr. Seuss. We know you're only nine, but we're thinking about all the great things that lie ahead of you."

Ms. Lebowitz read the story while her students sat crisscross applesauce on the edges of the carpet, their final days of being an age when they would regularly sit at their teachers' feet and be read a story. Symbols of the untangling, yet to come.

As the book neared its final page, the students reflected the mixture of excitement and nervousness they felt about publicly sharing their work. Lourdes covered her face with her poem and grabbed Ms. Lebowitz's legs. "Would you like me to read it for you?" Ms. Lebowitz asked. Lourdes nodded. Like most days, she wore a short-sleeved collared shirt tucked into jeans that were held up by an oversized silver belt buckle—a boyish outfit that contrasted sharply with her feminine features and frame.

"We're almost ready for the celebration," Ms. Schmidt began, "but we've gathered you guys here a little longer today because we have something important to talk about with you. A lot of you have been asking us if we're going to be back next year, and we wanted to let you know first that we are not coming back."

"Whaaaat?" the class yelled in unison.

"But we wanted to explain to you why and what we are going to be doing so that you understand first what is happening and why we will not be at Bancroft next year. I have a chance to work at a school that is not only teaching kids but also teaching teachers how to take all of the things I've learned here and be really great teachers for kids just like you guys. So I'm really sad to leave and I'm so proud of you. But I'll just be down the road—and I live a block away—so you'll still be seeing me around."

"I, on the other hand," said Ms. Lebowitz, "am leaving D.C. I'll be moving back to Boston to be close to my family. But also I was so inspired by all of the learning I saw, and it made me realize I wanted to go back to school. So, believe it or not, Ms. Lebowitz is going back to school next year so I can be an even better teacher. So even though I'll be really far away, you can bet I'll be visiting and I also love to write letters."

"If you leave, are you still going to visit?" asked Ernesto.

"You bet we will," Ms. Schmidt replied.

"If you leave," Harvey asked, just processing the news, "are you still going to visit?"

"We'll come back and see you," Ms. Lebowitz said, "and there's one more thing. Before we read your stories, we wanted to give each of you a book that Ms. Schmidt and I chose especially for you. And we want you to know how proud we are of all the great work you've done this year."

While Ms. Lebowitz spoke, Ms. Schmidt walked around the room, handing each child a gift-wrapped book and card. The titles they chose reflected the range of abilities in their classroom. For Elliott—the boy who had read 20 books the previous summer—they chose Norton Juster's *The Phantom Tollbooth*. For Rodger—the boy who had not understood how to even hold a book at the start of the year—they'd chosen Eric Carle's *The Mixed-Up Chameleon*. And for Harvey—the boy who'd taken up so much of their attention, worry, and love—they bought Mo Willems' *Leonardo the Terrible Monster*.

While Ms. Schmidt read Rodger the note she'd written in his book, the other children untied the bright blue ribbons around their books and thumbed through the pages. "This is so sweet of you!" said Ernesto. He kissed his book repeatedly and held it to his heart. "Hey—I think I'm going to cry. Thank you so much!"

Harvey turned to the note at the front of his oversized hardcover. "You are *our* little monster," it read. "And we adore you . . . and are so proud of the incredible work you've done this year. We can't wait to see what you do in the future!"

◊  ◊  ◊  **MV**  ◊  ◊  ◊

On the last day of the year at Mundo Verde, the glow of the previous week's expedition had been replaced by the long list of final housekeeping duties before summer. Most of the walls in Molly Howard's classroom were now bare, and milk crates filled with glue sticks and markers and strips of colored paper lined the base of the walls. While her co-teacher showed the class how to cut the points on some last-day-of-school crowns they were making—"I cut like thiiiis. I cut like thaaaat"—Molly met with each student a final time.

"We're going to spend a few minutes talking about your progress," Molly told Freya, who wore a red headband, leggings, and a long string of pearls. "When you came in here, do you remember that you could only count to 14?"

"I didn't know how to get to 15," she replied.

"I know! But now how high can you count?"

"I can count to 100 in both English and Spanish!"

"That's right! How did you get better?"

"I practiced with my grandmother in the car."

"That's such a good idea," Molly replied. She was perched at the end of a bench in the *Zocalo*, her long legs stretched out under the small table in front of her where Freya sat. "Do you also know that at the beginning of the year, you only knew 11 letters. How many do you know now?"

"All of them!"

"All of them. So much has happened this year. Let's write a letter to ourselves where we talk about what we're most proud of, and what we most want to work on. Will you do that with me?"

"I will."

Just beyond them, in Berenice's classroom, the Zebras were having a dance party on the rug. The students watched and waited as their teacher, her hair up in a colorful wrap, chose a new song.

The music of Shakira blared over the boombox's small speakers, and the students formed a five-year-old mosh pit. Stephen shook his arms and legs with abandon. Princess jumped up and down like a pogo stick. And Albert stuck close to his teacher, who giggled and thumped along with them. In a few days, she would be off to Madrid to study the architecture of Gaudí—she had an idea about next year's expedition she wanted to explore, and this was her chance to conduct some firsthand professional research, and have a personal adventure along the way.

A few rooms over, Dahlia and Kristin were absorbed in the latest list of logistical challenges. There was a survey of their parents they still needed to administer. Summer school was proving to be more complicated to arrange than they'd anticipated. They had a lot of people they still needed to hire. And they still had to finalize the agenda for the four-week summer institute at which they would lay the foundation for Year Two. As they spoke, they stood on either side of the whiteboard in their office, eyes fixed on its list of things to do like a playbook. "Last year there was a lot of excitement and urgency," Dahlia said. "But this year we'll have twice as many people, and everyone will be expecting a lot more differentiation. The bar is so much higher this year! It can't just be good—it has to be transformational."

"A *lot* has to happen in July," Kristin added. "We have to draft a calendar that really lets us set up a data cycle. And we can't expect people to be as forgiving of the things we didn't get right."

"Romey has a cool idea for our kickoff to the summer," Kristin added. "I think it's really going to help us solidify where we've been, and where we want to go next."

◊　◊　◊　**B**　◊　◊　◊

On the 180th and final day of the year—Rebecca Lebowitz's 25th birthday—the students of room 121 watched a movie while their teachers worked intently on the final tasks before summer. They had to have everything in their room boxed and labeled by the end of the day, and submit their final grades as well. The city's online student tracking and reporting system, however, was only working intermittently, which had slowed Ms. Schmidt's efforts to assign each child one of four letter grades for every standard in every subject: N—not introduced; B—beginning; D—developing; or S—secure.

When the Internet was working, Ms. Schmidt went down the list, rhythmically assigning numbers and letters for each child. A separate window on her computer was open with lists of all the data they'd collected, but she knew the figures by heart. A few of the standards themselves, however, felt less clear.

*"Describes logical connection between sentences in a paragraph of a text,"* she read out loud to her co-teacher. "I don't really know what that means so I'm going to give them the same thing I gave them last semester." Ms. Lebowitz nodded her approval; she was sorting through the students' folders and placing them on their desks. Her own desk was covered with various-sized homemade cards of thanks:

> *Ms. Schmidt is the best teacher in the 3rd Grade. You work hard to be a teacher.*

> *Dear Ms. Lebowitz, You are a very nice teacher and you have nice hair. You read very interesting books to us and that's great.*

> *I love Ms. Schmidt.*

That afternoon, the entire school gathered in the auditorium for a screening of their video. Although it was beautiful outside, it was sweltering inside—a reflection of the fact that the A/C and the heating were never quite in sync in this 90-year-old school.

"Bancroft? *Qué es Bancroft?*" asked two parents outside the school's front doors.

"It's our school," said a young boy. "Come on," Ms. Reid urged. "¡Venga, Venga!"

The camera entered the front doors and traveled through the building, down its checkerboard hallways, through its swinging doors, and past children on tricycles, children throwing confetti, and children passing a plastic globe down a line.

*See the champions*
*Take the field now*
*You define us*
*Make us feel proud*

The sounds from the children in the gymnasium drowned out the sound of the lyrics; Ms. Schmidt watched them watch themselves, these students who'd consumed her thoughts since August, and who reflected so fully the diversity of her city. She had spent the past several days trying intentionally to spend time with each of them before everyone scattered. "When you're not trying to teach them something," she once told me, "you have the most fun because we can just relate to each other as human beings, and feel less of this external pressure."

And then, anticlimactically, it was over. The children gathered their things, gave their teachers a final hug and ran outside to start their summers, already focused on what lay ahead. Ms. Schmidt sat in a chair with Lourdes draped across her lap. She whispered in her ear and rubbed her back, fighting back tears. Harvey walked up to Ms. Lebowitz, who took his head in her hands and stroked his cheeks.

"Take care of yourself," she said.

"Bye."

◊ ◊ ◊ **MV** ◊ ◊ ◊

Unlike the others, who set off in teams to look for the twigs, branches, and leaves they would weave together to capture the essence of their school, Kristin Scotchmer searched the ground around her, alone.

She could count on one hand the moments she'd been completely alone since deciding to start a new school from scratch. But now it was

June, and the inaugural year was over, and the staff of the Mundo Verde Bilingual Public Charter School was completing its last shared activity before the official start of the summer, when the size of their team would double, when they would transport all the records and wires and playthings and poster boards to a new building across town, and when the glow of what had just been accomplished would start to fade in exchange for a renewed anxiety of all the new challenges to be overcome.

Kristin leaned down and grabbed a branch, thin and moldable. This spot of Rock Creek Park was right next to the place she'd gone running all year to maintain her sense of balance—the only time of the week when no one could demand anything of her, and there was no problem to solve.

The teams returned to the clearing by the creek. Molly Howard was feeling ready for the year to be over. Berenice Pernalete was thinking about her summer adventure in Madrid that was just days away. And Dahlia Aguilar was steeling herself to be one of the ones to get in the water, because that's what her dad would have expected of his Dolly.

Before walking to the park from the school, which would soon revert to being just another floor in a downtown office building, Romey Pittman had shown them the artwork of Andy Goldsworthy. Each image she shared framed evanescent sculptures Goldsworthy made with only the materials nature provided: circles of reconstituted icicles; potholes along a stream filled with bright yellow dandelions; lines of white wool along a dark stone fence.

The group decided their sculpture would be a circle of branches, to reflect the spirit of the Oglala Lakota poem Dahlia had given them:

*In the Circle, we are all equal*
*When in the Circle.*
*No one is in front of you.*
*No one is behind you.*
*No one is above you.*
*No one is below you.*

Some bent stacks of sticks into shape, while others wove together the many gradients of green—grass, leaves, brush—into a long, crooked line that would, they decided, form a path to lay across the center of the circle. It was always the same, Romey thought as she watched these young women work, remembering the first cabin she and her husband had built, and then lost to a fire the night they moved in: you gather your materials, you consult your plans, you make your decisions, and then you build the house.

◊   ◊   ◊   **B**   ◊   ◊   ◊

The Bancroft Elementary School parade began in a small park at the confluence of five streets and three neighborhoods, and in the shadow of three different church spires. For months the weather had been cooler than usual, but by a mid-morning in June it was still hot enough to keep most of the adults huddled under the shade of the park's aging trees, each group swapping stories in a different mother tongue: Vietnamese, Spanish, Amharic, English. A police car idled at the base of the street that bore the name of the neighborhood it served—Mount Pleasant—and waited for the parade to begin.

As her teachers orchestrated the final arrangements—cheerleaders up front, drum and bugle corps to follow, and flag bearers representing every nation in the community picking up the rear—nine-year-old Lourdes adjusted the yellow "Nuestra Escuela" T-shirt across her slight shoulders and grabbed hold of the large, wide Bancroft banner with three other students. As they walked to the front of the line, past a sea of adults holding cameras and camcorders, Lourdes knew not to look for familiar faces. She wouldn't see her dad until later that summer, in Texas, and she had learned long ago it was best not to think about where Mami might be at any given moment. She watched the spinning lights at the top of the police car and imagined the parade was already over so she could be back on the soccer field, blazing down the sideline past all the boys to score another goal and show everyone how strong she really was.

The police car started crawling up the street, and the cheerleaders began their rhythmic chant: BAN-CROFT! The last remaining students and adults emerged from the shade of the trees to fall in line, while a phalanx of mothers with younger children formed an impromptu stroller brigade at the back.

Lourdes watched the people gathering in interest as the parade progressed down the street. Three heads poked out of a window above the 24-hour laundromat. A man with a lathered face got out of his chair to stand on the top step of the Pan American barbershop. An elderly woman sipped coffee from the porch of her aging Victorian, while younger children weaved their tricycles in between the foot traffic of the sidewalk.

As they reached the midway point of the street, Lourdes could see the white canopies of the neighborhood farmer's market—just past the Best World supermarket on one side of the street, and the blackened facade of the burned-out apartment building on the other.

Two blocks away, Zakiya Reid was preparing the back of the school for the parade's arrival. Parent volunteers set up the barbeque pit and sorted the hamburgers, hot dogs, and churros for quick cooking. Another group set up the moon bounce just beyond the dunking booth—her students always loved the chance to drop their principal into a tank of cold water.

Ms. Reid listened for the sound of the drums.

The year had not gone the way she had hoped. She'd endured a painful public challenge to her leadership. She'd struggled to gain support from her staff for a new style of classroom teaching. And she'd learned that two of her best in that new style, "the Two Rebeccas," would not be returning. Yet there were days like this that always seemed to come along at just the right time to remind her why she became an educator—days when a neighborhood's children and families would come together and remind each other that they were participating in the same dream: to unite all the children of a single community under a single roof in order to give them all an equal shot at success.

Kristin handed Berenice the leaves she had gathered and watched her stitch them together. This had been a year of seeing in Technicolor, and it had awakened in Kristin a vividness to her own being she didn't know was still there. The group finished the sculpture and she retreated to the side. They began moving it closer to the water, and she walked up to the small bridge that ran across the creek so she could view their actions from above. "I wanted it to go down the river," she told me afterward. "It felt like surrendering—like literally being OK with the work that has been done this year being over. And a recognition that we are all moving on."

Dahlia felt herself struggling to stay present in what everyone was doing. Just before they walked to the park, she had asked her teachers to compile a list of all the things the school should stop, start, and keep doing in Year Two. "It was really disappointing to see what they said," she confessed, "and I felt defensive and started to lose my mind and get all heated. I was angry that I let that understanding and frustration travel all the way through to this point of the year."

Then the group began to construct their design, and Dahlia noticed herself becoming more aware of her surroundings. "I chose to help out in the water because I'm scared of falling in general—even stairs freak me out. But I wanted to lean into the fear. I was having a really hard time. I couldn't move around very well. There were four of us, with everyone else watching from the shore or the bridge. I asked Berenice for help. She grabbed me by the hand. I don't do that very much. It's a problem. I didn't want it to float away, but no one else felt the same. I wanted it to stay and have people wonder what it was. Why let it break apart?"

Molly Howard liked the idea—to use what they created as a way to welcome the new staff members and help them understand what the school was all about. But she also felt personally distracted by the weeks ahead, and by her realization that she was ready to be done with it all for a while. "One group really wanted to do the branch wrapped with a gradient of leaves. The other wanted the branch wreath, originally to symbolize the world and then the full circle of us all together. We put it in the water and then we let it float away. It was like we were burying someone. It felt like a memorial service."

For Berenice Pernalete, it was a way to put some sort of action on a natural environment—to make visible something that was not randomly there. "After Romey showed us the pictures, we were all walking around and seeing everything differently. It was all art. The circle of life—us being united—feeling togetherness.

"We decided to put it in the water, and then we decided to just let it float away. When we let it go, I felt so touched—the year had come to an end, the children had passed through our classrooms and now we had to let them go.

"I imagined someone else in the park seeing this circle of branches floating down with the current. What would they say about it? What will people in the future say about our kids? I won't know the answer, but it's nice to wonder."

In July, just before she returned to her home city to prepare for the next stage of her professional and personal life, I met Rebecca Lebowitz at a D.C. coffee shop. It was a weekday afternoon, but the café was filled with folks of all shapes and sizes, hard at work, laptops glowing beside their oversized coffee cups and complimentary animal crackers.

The fact that the year was over hadn't sunk in for her yet. "This always happens," she explained. "I finish school and then I spend the next week trying to find things to do. Then I realize I can just sit around and relax. I've been packing stuff and selling furniture. But I'm really excited for what's next. I've known everything my whole life, and I'm trying really hard to not know this time. I don't want to think beyond it—I just want to love this year."

Before she returned to her packing, I asked her what she was most proud of during the 2011–2012 school year. She reached into her backpack, pulled out a wrinkled sheet of paper, and handed it to me.

It was a printout of Bancroft's reading proficiency rates by grade. These were the scores she and Ms. Schmidt had gathered at the beginning, middle, and end of the year—not the high-stakes tests that would have, had she stayed in DCPS, determined her effectiveness as a teacher.

And there it was. In a class that had just three of 60 students reading at grade level at the beginning of the year, Ms. Lebowitz and Ms. Schmidt had helped an additional 26 children do the same—an improvement of 43%.

No other grade was even close.

# Now What?

IN 1897, A 21-YEAR-OLD Italian immigrant named Angelo Patri began teaching in New York City's public school system. Forty-seven years later, he retired.

When Patri started teaching, the conventional wisdom was that children were to be seen and not heard, and Patri behaved accordingly. "I saw no individual faces," he wrote in his autobiography, *A Schoolmaster of the Great City*, "no distinct forms, just the great mass surging past."[1] As he gained experience, however, he realized his impersonal, disciplinarian style worked to great effect with his obedient students—and did almost nothing to reach his troubled ones. For those youngsters in particular, and for all of the children in general, what brought the classroom to life were his personal stories, his students' stories, and challenging work that was directly applicable to the communities in which they lived. "Conduct," he realized, "not the ability to recite lessons, was the real test of learning and the sign of culture."[2]

Angelo Patri's artful intuitions of a century ago have since been confirmed by generations of scientists. The 100 billion neurons in our brain—each as complicated as a city, and each with an average of 10,000 connections—are not, as was once thought, fixed and immutable. Instead, we now know the brain is malleable, and that it is molded most formatively by what it experiences. "Everything that happens to us affects the way the brain develops," says Dan Siegel, a clinical professor of psychiatry at UCLA. "The brain is a social organ, made to be in relationship. What happens *between* brains has a great deal to do with what happens *within* each individual brain . . . [And] the physical architecture of the brain changes according to where we direct our attention and what we practice doing."[3]

Over the course of the year I spent embedded in two Washington, D.C. classrooms—one a group of kindergartners in a first-year charter school, the other a group of third-graders in a 90-year-old neighborhood school—I observed what children practiced and where adults directed their attention. I watched five-year-olds script, design, and produce a film about the migratory pattern of the Monarch butterfly—and then grow into a fuller sense of themselves as a result. And I witnessed talented teachers diagnose the myriad needs of their students—intellectual, social, emotional—and then struggle to meet those needs amidst a larger policy climate that prioritized only one piece of the developmental puzzle.

My reasons for writing *Our School* were both personal and professional. I wanted to see what it felt like to be a teacher in 2012, and to compare those experiences to my own teaching career, which ended in 2000. I wanted to follow a few parents who were trying to choose a school for their children for the first time, and see to what extent their experiences mirrored my wife's and my search for our own son. And most of all I wanted to put a human face on the modern landscape of school choice, which has become so polarized and politicized as to render almost all of its central characters in two-dimensional terms.

Other things I intended just as intentionally *not* to do. I did not set out to compare charter and district schools in order to render a verdict on which model was "good" and which was "bad." I did not assume our national culture of testing would be revealed as purely harmful or harmless. And I did not expect to discover whether school choice was definitively aiding or destroying the social fabric of our communities. On these questions and others, I agree with former Chinese premier Zhou Enlai, who, when asked by reporters in 1971 to offer his assessment of the impact of the French Revolution of 1789, said: "It is still too soon to say."

One thing I did know was that whatever I observed in those two classrooms over the course of the 2011–2012 school year would paint an accurate, albeit partially painted, picture of public schooling as it is.

Now that the year is over, I want to add my thoughts on what it ought to be.

First, **our teachers need to be prepared and supported differently.**
Too many of our current teacher certification programs, whether they're
in public universities or private organizations, offer incomplete path-
ways to the profession. Some overvalue subject expertise and behavior
management skills to the exclusion of nearly everything else. Others act
as though teaching is a purely academic endeavor, and that the social
and cultural contexts of the communities in which teachers work do not
require deep consideration and understanding. And not enough programs proceed with a clear sense of the difference between *teaching* quality—strong instruction that enables a wide range of students to learn
and thrive—and *teacher* quality, which refers to the bundle of personal
traits, skills, and understandings an individual brings to their work.

Notably, every teacher I observed over the course of writing *Our
School* said she felt unprepared for the actual challenges of the classroom, and for understanding how to meet the myriad needs of her
students. And every one described spending late nights reading books
or searching for resources online—a result of the sizable disconnect
between our timeworn notions of what teaching looks like, and their
everyday experiences of what it now requires.

Another issue that needs remedying is the high rate of teacher
turnover, which is anathema to the establishment of a healthy, sustainable culture. Bancroft, for example, was losing an average of 25% of
its staff every year, and Mundo Verde's inaugural faculty was almost
entirely made up of first- or second-year teachers. More significantly,
by the time *Our School* was released, only one of the four teachers
I observed—Mundo Verde's Berenice Pernalete—was still working
at the same school. Rebecca Lebowitz is now in Boston, getting her
EdD; Molly Howard is there now, too, helping set up the elementary
school program for a charter school in the Expeditionary Learning
network; and Rebecca Schmidt is teaching at a charter school in D.C.
It's encouraging that all four of these talented women still work in
education—and it's telling that the reason three of them left their previous posts was because they felt it had become impossible to do the
job effectively and sustainably. And no wonder, when one considers
that teachers today are being asked to customize their instruction for
every individual child, and do so with minimal experience or relevant
training. "If you are a student in an American classroom today," writes

Celine Coggins, founder and CEO of Teach Plus, "the odds that you will be assigned to an inexperienced teacher are higher than they have ever been. In fact, right now there are more first-year teachers in American classrooms than teachers at any other experience level."[4]

The response to this "capacity gap" is not to stop hiring young teachers or keep employing old ones, but to start ensuring that all teachers can diagnose and meet the developmental needs of every child. And the good news is there are already valuable models we can look to as our guides.

Take America's medical schools. As any M.D. knows, different schools have different strengths and weaknesses. But one thing every medical school shares is the belief that a strong professional training is built on a dual foundation of two courses: Anatomy and Physiology.

In education, as Yale University professor (and M.D.) James Comer has noted, no similar consensus exists. Worse still, most programs give short shrift to the two most important things a teacher needs to know: how children learn, and how they develop.

Think about that for a second. Our country's teacher preparation programs, by and large, pay little attention to how well prospective educators understand the emotional and developmental needs of the children they propose to teach. But there's nothing preventing these programs from heeding Dr. Comer's advice and adapting the med school model by establishing a similar two-course foundation for all prospective educators: *Developmental Sciences*, which would provide a foundation in the cognitive, social, emotional, ethical, physical, and linguistic needs of children; and *Learning Sciences*, which would give teachers a solid foundation in understanding how people learn.

Meanwhile, to better support the millions of teachers who are already in classrooms across the country, we must craft evaluation programs that honor the art *and* science of teaching. One of the few things all sides seem to agree on is that teacher evaluation systems are in need of an extreme makeover; for too long, they've been little more than pro forma stamps of approval, and they've done little to nothing to help teachers get better.

In too many places, however, efforts are underway to craft systems that disregard the art of teaching in favor of the (misunderstood) science of measurement. These sorts of systems are more about pushing people out than lifting them up, and they continue to act as though student acquisition of specific, tested academic skills (as opposed to their overall intellectual, social, and emotional growth) is the preeminent measure of an effective teacher.

We should blow them all up and start over.

A prerequisite of any evaluation system should be its capacity to help teachers improve the quality of their professional practice via shared, strategic inquiry into what is and isn't working for children in their classrooms. These new systems shouldn't be afraid of quantitative analysis, just as they shouldn't devalue qualitative measures. And they should assess teachers by their effectiveness to support children across the entire developmental continuum.

There are several illustrative efforts underway. If you're a policymaker, take a close look at what they're doing in places like Montgomery County, Maryland, where a program called Peer Assistance Review, or PAR, uses senior teachers to mentor both newcomers and struggling veterans.[5] And if you're a teacher, consider getting certified by the National Board for Professional Teaching Standards (nbpts.org), a teacher-run organization that uses a performance-based, multiple-measure, peer-reviewed process to identify and acknowledge the definitive standards of accomplished teaching and the process by which the profession can certify whether or not a teacher meets those standards.

It will always be true, in teaching and in the natural world, that not everything can be measured, just as it's true that there are ways to measure aspects of teaching and learning that go a lot deeper than basic-skills test scores. The challenge is to find the balance between the elusive but evergreen art of teaching, and the emerging but illustrative science of the brain. We can do both.

Second, **our students (and our schools) need to be assessed differently.** Don't be fooled by the public pronouncements about whether your child's school is successful or unsuccessful, whether it is high-performing or low-performing, or whether the achievement gap there is growing or shrinking. All of those buzzwords are shorthand for the same thing: reading and math scores.

This is a shell game we have been playing for too long. We use partial information to pronounce complete judgment on whether a given

reform effort is working or not. And, more importantly, we allow ourselves to assign credit or blame in ways that correspond to a political
timetable.

In reality, it's not that simple. As the late Ted Sizer wrote in his clas-
sic about teaching, *Horace's Compromise*: "True standards of intellect—
even those of a restless, noisy adolescent—do not lend themselves
wholly to quickly collected, precise, standard measurement. We need
to devise clusters of instruments to probe our students' ability to think
resourcefully about important things. Indeed, we need time to reflect
deeply on what we mean by 'think resourcefully' and what we feel are
the most 'important things.'"[6]

Reading and math scores, in other words, are valuable—and over-
valued. And until we devise those clusters of instruments Sizer was
calling for, we'll continue putting our teachers and principals in an
impossible position.

The good news is we know more than we think we do about what
a great learning environment looks like. Prior to writing *Our School*, I
edited a collection of 50 people's stories about their own most powerful learning experiences[7]—the idea being that if we could mine our *personal* memories for shared insights that could enhance our *professional*
lives, we should do so.

What I discovered is that when you ask people to reflect on their
most powerful learning experience—regardless of whether it took
place in school or out of school, and regardless of what age they
were when it happened—what emerges is a clear, shared set of core
characteristics.

As it turns out, the ideal learning environment for all of us is, to
differing degrees, challenging, engaging, relevant, supportive, and experiential. And not surprisingly, the timeless value of those conditions
is supported by the latest research on the brain. "Learners of all ages
are more motivated when they can see the usefulness of what they are
learning and when they can use that information to do something that
has an impact on others—especially their local community," reported
a coalition of scholars in the 1999 report, *How People Learn*.[8] Case West-
ern's James Zull, a professor of biology and the author of *The Art of
Changing the Brain*, concurs: "Learning depends on experience, but it
also requires reflection, developing abstractions, and active testing of

our abstractions. . . . So we might say that our best chance to help another person learn is to find out what they want, what they care about."[9]

This is what Angelo Patri was urging us to do for children back in 1917. "The average parent thinks of education largely in terms of books," he wrote. "Parents have been trained, as have the teachers, to think of school as a place where the children are made to obey, to memorize, made to repeat lessons. . . . [But] you must not think too much of arithmetic, and rules and dates and examinations, for these are not teaching; the children don't grow because of them. They grow because of their contact with you, the best that you know and feel."[10]

So what would an assessment system that honors the art and science of learning need to look like? I believe it would involve fewer high-stakes external assessments like the one that was administered at Bancroft—and whose results were not even known until the following school year (how helpful is that?). And clearly, it would be aligned with the same developmental framework for teachers I just described.

To get the ball rolling, I have a scorecard to propose—call it the "ABCs of School Success." Bearing Ted Sizer's recommendations in mind, it provides both structure and freedom by identifying five universal measurement categories, and then letting individual schools chose which data points to track under each category.

## 1. Achievement

If there is a bottom line in schools today, it's that educators must do whatever it takes to close the achievement gap. To do so effectively and fully, however, schools must expand their measures for determining what "achievement" actually *is*, and what closing the gap actually *means*.

I agree with University of Wisconsin-Madison professor Gloria Ladson-Billings, who suggests that what the United States has is not an achievement gap, but an *educational debt* that has accumulated over centuries of denied access to education and employment, and been reinforced by deepening levels of poverty and resource inequalities in schools which continue to leave children of color and the poor behind.[11]

What, then, would an expanded definition of achievement need to look like—one that could be part of a larger strategy to pay down our generations-old educational debt? I believe the following are all critical:

- Teachers and administrators are skilled in their use of feedback—both quantitative and qualitative—to diagnose and meet the developmental needs of their students.
- The school has identified aspirational "habits of mind and being" for students, and adopted assessment measures to track student development of these habits over time.
- The school uses assessments that require students to conduct research and scientific investigations, solve complex real-world problems in mathematics, and defend their ideas orally and in writing.
- The school provides learning support programs that address individual student needs and ensure that all students are placed in an optimal position to succeed.
- The school has developed a curriculum that is challenging, experiential, accessible, and relevant to a diverse student population.
- The school has programs, personnel, and services in place that are designed to help the least-advantaged children receive the additional supports they need to come to school ready to learn.

If each school identified between three and ten different data points to assess their overall learning environment, we might start to see "achievement" as a broader set of measures, and evaluate the full extent to which we are supporting the young people we serve.

## 2. Balance

We all seek balance in our lives. The search for it is a fundamental part of the human condition. Imagine how much more enjoyable—and effective—our schools would be if we assessed them, in part, through this prism.

As it turns out, adopting a more integrated approach to learning is as important for our minds as it is for our souls. As Dan Siegel explains, "We want to help our children become better integrated so they can use their whole brain in a coordinated way. We want them to be *horizontally integrated*, so that their left-brain logic can work well with their right-brain emotion. We also want them to be *vertically integrated*, so that the physically higher parts of the brain, which let them thoughtfully consider their actions, work well with the lower parts, which are more concerned with instinct, gut reactions, and survival."[12]

To create more balanced school environments, schools should consider the extent to which:

- Students have sufficient, regular opportunities for enrichment activities like dance, art, physical education, and so on.
- Effective vehicles are in place to help the school routinely communicate with its families and the larger community— and vice versa.
- Teachers from different disciplines communicate with, work together, and support one another's professional practice on a regular basis.
- Teachers incorporate both formative (instructional) and summative (evaluative) assessments into their evaluations of student progress.
- Teachers routinely solicit, listen to, reflect on, and integrate student feedback into their work.

Additional measures in this category could include parent, student, and teacher attitudinal surveys. Other existing data points could be useful as well, such as staff absenteeism rates (healthy schools have low ones). The point is not to dictate the individual measures, but to observe what schools discover as they start to experiment with the scorecard. As veteran educator Parker Palmer puts it, "Teaching and learning, done well, are done not by disembodied intellects: they are done by whole persons whose intellects cannot be disentangled from the complex of faculties held together by the heart. And as the neurobiologist Candace Pert has pointed out, the *brain* is located under the cranium, whereas the *mind* is distributed throughout the body. To teach *as* a whole person *to* the whole person is not to lose one's professionalism; it is to take it to a deeper level."[13]

## 3. Climate

"For almost a hundred years," explains Jonathan Cohen, director of the National School Climate Center, "educators have appreciated the importance of school climate—the quality or character of school life. We can all remember childhood moments when we felt particularly safe (or unsafe) in school, when we felt particularly connected to a caring adult (or frighteningly alone), when we felt particularly engaged in meaningful learning (or not). However, school climate is larger than any one person's experience. When people work together, a group process emerges that is bigger than any one person's actions."[14]

A school's overall climate is an essential indicator of its overall health. So let's start insisting that all schools measure it. One possibility would be to use the Comprehensive School Climate Inventory (CSCI),[15] a research-based needs assessment that provides immediate feedback on how students, parents, and school personnel perceive their school's overall environment for learning. Other useful measures exist, and new ones would emerge over time. And in this and the other categories, an ongoing role of the federal government would be to share insights about measurement and the use of the scorecard across states and communities, so information could be funneled back throughout the system and create a reciprocal flow of information that improves the quality of all schools.

## 4. Democratic Practices

In a school setting, cultivating democratic practices doesn't mean turning the asylum over to the inmates. To create a climate where people feel both empowered and protected, you don't start by just telling everyone that they're free. You do, however, make helping people learn how to exercise freedom responsibly a foundational goal.[16]

Before that vision can become a reality, we must encourage educators to ensure that the central elements of our social covenant are also in place in our schools: a clear sense of structure and shared identity on one hand, and an unwavering commitment to individual expression on the other.

To help create such environments, we should gauge the extent to which our schools are equipping young people with the understanding, motivation, and skills they need to become active, visible contributors to the common good.

Schools can do so by considering the extent to which:

- Administrators have established structures and/or accorded meaningful roles in decision-making to students, parents, staff, and community members.
- Students are routinely encouraged throughout the curriculum to agree and disagree honestly and respectfully.
- The school encourages people to model democratic principles, practices, and policies in their daily work and interactions with others.
- The school's mission and vision statements clearly address the democratic purposes of education.
- The community is committed to ensuring that religious liberty rights are protected for persons of all faiths and none.
- Students understand how to participate in the political process and institutions that shape public policy.
- Students are given regular opportunities to take public action on personally meaningful issues and concerns.

Institutions like public schools help make up the *visible* infrastructure of democracy. They do not fulfill their purpose, however, unless they (public, charter, or otherwise) equip children with the *invisible* infrastructure—the habits of the heart—that can guide them through college, career, and citizenship.

## 5. Equity

To ensure greater equity—by which I mean reducing the predictive value sociocultural and economic characteristics have on student success, motivation, and engagement in school—we must improve the performance of our public schools and strengthen the effectiveness of our civic activism at the same time.

These challenges are interdependent, and will remain so. Indeed, the poorest and least fortunate in our country are not just the least likely to succeed academically—they are also the most disenfranchised from our political process.

Therefore, to measure their commitment to equity (of resources and opportunity), school leaders should consider tracking the extent to which:

- The aspirations, strengths, and weaknesses of each student are known by at least one member of the school staff.
- The school actively collaborates with its students' families as partners in the students' education.
- The school's pupil nondiscrimination policies and complaint procedures are comprehensive and effective.
- Staff and students are aware of these policies and complaint procedures and act in accordance with them.
- Teachers know and can use a rich variety of strategies to identify and accommodate individual learning profiles and strengthen each student's ability to learn in diverse ways.
- The school provides its students with equal access to highly qualified teachers; strong curricular opportunities; books, materials, and equipment (including science labs and computers); and adequate facilities.
- The school believes passionately in empowering students, families, and community members to be contributing participants in their education, their community, and the diverse society in which we live.

Six decades ago, the U.S. Supreme Court's unanimous ruling in *Brown v. Board of Education* captured the most hopeful strains of the American narrative: working within a system of laws to extend the promise of freedom, more fairly and fully, to each succeeding generation. "In the field of public education," the Court wrote, "the doctrine of 'separate but equal' has no place," and the opportunity to learn "is a right which must be made available to all on equal terms."

If we are serious about fulfilling the decades-old promise of the *Brown* decision, we have to invest in a clear, flexible, and balanced system for evaluating and improving our nation's schools. I think this scorecard—or something like it—would be a great place to start.

Finally, **our democracy needs to be seen as something we do, not something we have.** When it comes to a nascent experiment like school choice, we have within us the capacity to turn an open marketplace of learning options into something creative and regenerative. But there is nothing automatic about it. Choice by itself leads to nothing. As John Dewey said, the purpose of education is not to merely grant children freedom of activity or choice or movement, but to empower them with the freedom to engage in *intelligent* activity, to make *intelligent* choices, and to exercise *intelligent* self-control in identifying, and then acting on, their unique strengths and interests. And so it is with us.

Consequently, I worry about what could happen if too many of us simply assume that the invisible hand of the modern school marketplace—or, worse still, the incentivizing hand of the modern school official—is a sufficient strategy for ensuring that all children receive equal access to a high-quality public education. And I take seriously the warnings of scholars like Harvard's Michael Sandel, who has urged us to think much more carefully about the role market-based thinking should have—scratch that, *does* have—in our lives.

"Markets don't just allocate goods," Sandel writes in *What Money Can't Buy: The Moral Limits of Markets.* "They also express and promote certain attitudes towards the goods being exchanged." And what has occurred over the past 30 years is that without quite realizing it, we have shifted from *having* a market economy to *being* a market society. "The difference is this: A market economy is a tool—a valuable and effective tool—for organizing productive activity. A market society is a way of life in which market values seep into every aspect of human endeavor. It's a place where social relations are made over in the image of the market."[17]

Anyone who has closely followed the *sturm und drang* of American school reform over the past decade has seen evidence of what Sandel is discussing. Indeed, the growing reliance on—and resistance to—data-driven decision-making is a direct result of an ascendant technocratic faith in applying scientific rigor to the previously opaque art of teaching and learning. Economist Gary Becker sums up this thinking well when he asserts: "The economic approach is a comprehensive one that is applicable to all human behavior, be it behavior involving money prices or imputed shadow prices, repeated or infrequent decisions, large or minor decisions, emotional or mechanical ends, rich or poor persons, men or women, adults or children, brilliant or stupid persons, patients or therapists, businessmen or politicians, teachers or students."[18]

That's a mouthful, and it captures the sea change Sandel wants us to see. Whereas in the not-too-distant past, economic thinking was restricted to economic topics—inflation, investment, trade—today it is being used to outline a new science of human behavior: one that assumes modern society will work best when human beings are allowed to weigh the costs and benefits of all things (including where to send their children to school), and then choose whatever they believe will yield the greatest personal benefit.

The part of me that agrees with that logic is the part that supports the basic idea of school choice. After all, we have tolerated a system of unequal opportunity in this country for too long, and there's undeniable merit in the argument that one's zip code should not become one's destiny. In theory, school choice is a democratizing force that gives everyone the same chance at a high-quality education, and empowers each family to set its own "shadow prices"—the imaginary values that are implicit in the alternatives we face and the choices we make—and then make their own decisions about where to send their children to school. As one popular slogan puts it, "MY CHILD, MY CHOICE."

Who could argue with that?

But here's where it gets complicated. In the end, should we define public education as a public or a private good? Will our efforts to unleash self-interest (which is, after all, what the economist seeks to economize) strengthen or weaken the connective tissue of our civic life? And will the current trajectory of the charter school movement unleash a virtuous cycle of reforms that improves all schools, or merely add another layer in our historically inequitable system of schooling? As British sociologist Richard Titmuss explains, "The ways in which society organizes and structures its social institutions can encourage or discourage the altruistic in man, foster integration or alienation," and strengthen or "erode the sense of community."[19]

Our changing notion of community should be the central concern of anyone who cares about school choice. To transform our communities, however, we need more than just new ideas about how to organize our schools or prepare our teachers or assess our students; we need a shared emotional commitment to those ideas, and to one another, that we can translate into new norms of behavior. As *The New Yorker*'s Atul Gawande explains in a 2013 article about innovation, ideas alone do not lead to behavior change: "People follow the lead of other people they know and trust when they decide whether to take it up. Every change requires effort, and the decision to make that effort is a social process."

That social process is what allows people to adopt new norms of behavior. And "to create new norms, you have to understand people's existing norms and barriers to change. You have to understand what's getting in their way."[20]

This is not what we do. Instead, we sidestep the slower process of co-creating new norms in favor of the quicker path of mandating new behaviors. But as school change expert Michael Fullan points out, the key to real systems change is building *collective capacity*, which he defines as "generating the emotional commitment and the technical expertise that no amount of individual capacity working alone can come close to matching."[21] Potential innovations like smaller classrooms, in other words, mean nothing unless the move is coordinated with relevant professional development for teachers to help them employ new strategies. Establishing national standards means nothing if the end result is merely more national exams and less high-quality, locally driven assessments that use those standards as a common frame. And new teacher evaluation systems mean nothing unless the teachers who will be evaluated in them feel a sense of ownership over the new processes that will determine their professional fates.

How we *feel* about a new idea shapes how, and if, we apply it. No shortcuts. No excuses.

Unfortunately, as Gawande explains, "we've become enamored of ideas that spread as effortlessly as ether. We want frictionless, 'turnkey' solutions to the major difficulties of the world. We prefer instructional videos to teachers, drones to troops, incentives to institutions. People and institutions can feel messy and anachronistic. They introduce, as the engineers put it, uncontrolled variability." So we try to sidestep that variability altogether, which is the equivalent of recalling the first half of the famous quote by Winston Churchill—"Democracy is the worst form of government"—and conveniently forgetting the second half—"except all the others that have been tried."

American democracy was intended to generate, not suppress, the energy created by conflict; our differences of opinion are not the problem. But the only way our ideological dividing lines can lead to "civil friction" is if we allow the people and organizations we disagree with to become more than mere obstacles to greater efficiency, or stock characterizations of good or evil. "Our diversity consists only in part of demographic differences such as race, ethnicity, and social class," writes Parker Palmer. "Equally important are the wildly different lenses through which we see, think, and believe."[22]

I hope *Our School* has helped you develop a deeper feel for how differently we all see, think, and believe. The things we talk about when we talk about school reform—charter schools, testing, teachers, choice—are not black-and-white concepts; they are myriad shades of gray. That means the only chance we have of developing a system of schools worthy of our children is if we step out of our righteous certainty and lean into our empathetic openness. And the only way we'll do that is if we're willing, amidst the "uncontrolled variability" of ourselves, our colleagues, and our institutions, to talk through our deepest differences respectfully, openly, and with urgent patience. As the American author and activist Terry Tempest Williams puts it, "The human heart is the first home of democracy. It is where we embrace our questions. Can we be equitable? Can we be generous? Can we listen with our whole beings, not just our minds, and offer our attention rather than our opinions? And do we have enough resolve in our hearts to act courageously, relentlessly, without giving up—ever—trusting our fellow citizens to join with us in our determined pursuit of a living democracy?"[23]

No excuses. No shortcuts.

Not that long ago, I met up with Yolanda Hood for the first time in several months. Hunter was halfway through his first year at Mary McLeod Bethune, and I wanted to hear how it was going.

"It's a nice school," she said. "Hunter loves it. I've had moments where I wondered if it was really the best choice, but everyone there knows his name and what he's like, and his one-year-old sister never wants to leave when we drop him off each morning."

Still, she planned to attend the Charter School Expo again the following January. "I found out there's going to be a brand-new Hebrew school coming out, and there was talk of an Arabic school, too. I want to see for myself what they're all about. His education is too important to do anything less."

# Acknowledgments

I first decided I wanted to become a teacher because of Craig Werner.

When I entered his classes at UW-Madison, I was a directionless teenager in search of . . . something. Then he played the title track of Thelonius Monk's *Misterioso*, and we listened intently as Monk purposely misplayed a few keys in the opening. "Why do you think he would do that?" he asked us. And just like that, I felt like I understood what learning was about.

I wrote *Our School* to try and honor the profession Craig first made me want to enter 20 years ago, and that I have had the privilege of practicing and observing in schools across the country ever since. I couldn't have done so unless a small group of educators decided to take a leap of faith and welcome me fully into their lives and classrooms.

By definition, a leap of faith involves a fair amount of risk. For Dahlia Aguilar and Kristin Scotchmer, the risk was to invite an outsider into the inner circle of their dream school's inaugural year of existence—and not pick and choose what I got to see. For Molly Howard, it was allowing a writer to sit and watch her first year as a teacher, and record those moments in a permanent record she would quickly outgrow. For Berenice Pernalete, it was agreeing to be written about by someone who didn't speak the language she used exclusively during the day, and trusting that the final product would still reflect the fullness of her work. For Rebecca Lebowitz, Rebecca Schmidt, and Zakiya Reid, it was deciding to speak candidly about their dreams and disappointments at a time when many of their colleagues feel that one's honesty will only lead to one's dismissal. And for Karen Copeland, Yolanda Hood, Romey Pittman, and Valerie Flores, it was believing that my motive was to humanize their memories and experiences, not distort them.

I am forever grateful to the trust these women placed in me, and I hope the feeling that I represented their efforts truthfully will endure over time.

Once the manuscript was finished, several friends and colleagues provided close readings that helped me employ my words more judiciously. Katherine Bradley and Maya Soetoro-Ng, in particular, gave detailed feedback and much-needed encouragement. Toni Conklin, Zac Chase, Darcy Bedortha, Scott Nine, Cornelia Spelman, Reg Gibbons, Knox Johnstone, Aileen Chaltain, John Carter, Charles Haynes, and Christopher Wilson helped me refine the narrative as well. And my editor, Brian Ellerbeck, eloquently reflected back at me the things I had intended to convey—and the areas where I had missed the mark. Thanks to all of you for the perspective and the improvements.

When it came time to write, I found refuge among both my colleagues at Ashoka and the coffees at my neighborhood diner, The Coupe. Thank you for enduring my sticky-note-covered office walls and hours-long booth visits, respectively.

In the end, this project would not have been possible without the support of the NoVo Foundation, which granted me the freedom to embed myself in two schools for an entire school year. I am grateful for the trust of Jennifer and Peter Buffett, and for the belief that Robert Sherman and Pamela McVeagh-Lally had in me in the first place.

Over the past few years, I've been lucky enough to forge a friendship with Sir Ken Robinson. Ken's gift, as his books and talks have made clear to hundreds of millions of people around the world, is the ability to describe education both as it is and as it ought to be. It's a great honor to have his name alongside mine on this book.

Finally, although I dedicated *Our School* to Leo and Izzy, it's for their mother, Sarah Margon, just as much. Whereas other people see bits and pieces of whatever it is I'm working on, Sarah is part of the entire construction process. Her willingness to listen to each new idea or story—over chaotic breakfasts, date-night dinners, or homebound glasses of wine—and her determination to always give it to me straight, ensures that I get rid of the fluff and stick to the story.

"It's smart," she said to me when she finished reading the whole thing for the first time.

It's the greatest compliment I could receive.

# Notes

## Chapter 2

1. Frederick M. Hess, "Acknowledging the Trade-Offs," via "Are Top Students Getting Short Shrift?" *New York Times*, October 2, 2011. www.nytimes. com/roomfordebate/2011/10/02/are-top-students-getting-short-shrift/ acknowledging-the-trade-offs-in-differentiation

2. Carol Ann Tomlinson, "Done Well, Differentiation Works," via "Are Top Students Getting Short Shrift?" *New York Times*, October 2, 2011. www.nytimes. com/roomfordebate/2011/10/02/are-top-students-getting-short-shrift/ done-well-differentiation-works

3. Lisa Delpit, *Other People's Children: Cultural Conflict in the Classroom* (New York: The New Press, 2006), p. xiii.

4. David Sloan Wilson, *The Neighborhood Project* (New York & Boston: Little, Brown & Company, 2011), pp. 243–244.

5. Paul Tough, *How Children Succeed: Grit, Curiosity, and the Hidden Power of Character* (Boston & New York: Houghton Mifflin, 2012), pp. 17, 21.

## Chapter 3

1. Michael J. Petrilli, "The Fastest Gentrifying Neighborhoods in the United States," *Flypaper*, June 11, 2012. www.edexcellence.net/commentary/education-gadfly-daily/flypaper/2012/the-fastest-gentrifying-neighborhoods-in-the-united-states.html

2. *Quality Schools: Every Child, Every School, Every Neighborhood: An Analysis of Location and Performance in Washington, DC.* IFF (January 2012).

3. The Equal Protection Clause comes at the end of the first section of the Fourteenth Amendment. It says: "All persons born or naturalized in the United States, and subject to the jurisdiction thereof, are citizens of the United States and of the State wherein they reside. No State shall make or enforce any law which shall abridge the privileges or immunities of citizens of the United States; nor shall any State deprive any person of life, liberty, or property, without due process of law; *nor deny to any person within its jurisdiction the equal protection of the laws"* (emphasis added).

4. *Brown v. Board of Education*, 347 U.S. 483 (1954).

5. *San Antonio Independent School District v. Rodriguez*, 411 U.S. 1 (1973).

6. Lewis Mumford, *The City in History.* (San Diego: Harcourt, 1961), p. 8.

7. Ibid., p. 31.

8. Ibid., p. 9.

9. Jane Jacobs, *The Death and Life of Great American Cities.* (New York: Random House, 1961), p. viii.

10. Scott W. Berg, *Grand Avenues: The Story of Pierre Charles L'Enfant, the French Visionary Who Designed Washington, DC.* (New York: Vintage Books, 2007), p. 79.

## Chapter 4

1. David Eagleman, *Incognito: The Secret Lives of the Brain* (New York: Vintage Books, 2011), p. 48.

2. John Dewey, *Experience and Education.* (New York: Touchstone, 1938), p. 71.

## Chapter 7

1. www.edexcellence.net/commentary/education-gadfly-daily/common-core-watch/2013/trust-but-verify-the-real-lessons-of-campbells-law.html

2. Valerie Strauss, "Moco Schools Chief Calls for Three-Year Moratorium on Standardized Testing." *Washington Post*, December 10, 2012. www.washingtonpost.com/blogs/answer-sheet/wp/2012/12/10/moco-schools-chief-calls-for-three-year-moratorium-on-standardized-testing/

3. Cienna Madrid, "More Seattle Schools Join Boycott of MAP Test." *The Stranger,* January 21, 2103. www.slog.thestranger.com/slog/archives/2013/01/21/schools-national-educators-support-garfield-high-map-standardize-test-boycott

4. Morgan Smith, "Senate Education Leader Files Testing Bill." *Texas Tribune,* January 22, 2013. www.texastribune.org/2013/01/22/senate-education-leader-files-testing-bill

5. Stephanie Banchero, "Seattle Teachers Protest Exams." *Wall Street Journal,* January 25, 2013. online.wsj.com/news/articles/SB10001424127887323854904578264253178260028

6. Malcolm Gladwell, *The Tipping Point: How Little Things Can Make a Big Difference* (New York & Boston: Little, Brown & Co.), p. 7.

## Chapter 9

1. Daniel Koretz, *Measuring Up: What Educational Testing Really Tells Us* (Cambridge, MA: Harvard University Press, 2009), p. 49.

2. Ibid., p. 55.

3. Ibid., p. 57.

4. Ibid., pp. 38, 120.

## Epilogue

1. Angelo Patri, *A Schoolmaster of the Great City* (New York & London: The New Press, 2007), p. 17.

2. Ibid., p. 9.

3. Daniel J. Siegel & Tina Payne Bryson, *The Whole Brain Child: 12 Revolutionary Strategies to Nurture Your Child's Developing Mind* (New York: Delacorte Press 2011), pp. 8, 99, 122.

4. Teach Plus, *Great Expectations: Teachers' Views on Elevating the Profession* (October 2012), p. 3.

5. See, for example, Michael Winerip, "Helping Teachers Help Themselves," *New York Times*, June 5, 2011. www.nytimes.com/2011/06/06/education/06oneducation.html?pagewanted=all&_r=3&

6. Theodore R. Sizer, *Horace's Compromise: The Dilemma of the American High School* (Boston: Houghton Mifflin & Co., 2004), p. 228.

7. Sam Chaltain, ed., *Faces of Learning: 50 Powerful Stories of Defining Moments in Education* (Hoboken, NJ: Wiley, 2011).

8. National Research Council, *How People Learn: Brain, Mind, Experience and School* (Washington, DC: National Academy Press, 1999), p. 61.

9. James E. Zull, *The Art of Changing the Brain: Enriching the Practice of Teaching by Exploring the Biology of Learning* (Sterling, VA: Stylus Publishing, 2002), pp. 18, 48.

10. Patri, pp. 33, 12.

11. Gloria Ladson-Billings, "From the Achievement Gap to the Education Debt: Understanding Achievement in U.S. Schools," *Educational Researcher 35*, no. 10 (2006): 3–12.

12. Siegel & Bryson, p. 7.

13. Parker J. Palmer, *Healing the Heart of Democracy* (San Francisco: Jossey-Bass, 2011), p. 128.

14. See, for example, www.schoolclimate.org

15. www.schoolclimate.org/programs/csci.php

16. For a great example of a school that has created a successful democratic learning community, check out the 10-part video series, ayearatmissionhill.com.

17. Michael J. Sandel, *What Money Can't Buy: The Moral Limits of Markets* (New York: Farrar, Strauss & Giroux, 2012), p. 10.

18. Cited in Sandel, p. 49.

19. Cited in Sandel, p. 124.

20. Atul Gawande, "Slow Ideas," *The New Yorker*, July 29, 2013. www.newyorker.com/reporting/2013/07/29/130729fa_fact_gawande

21. Michael Fullan, *All Systems Go: The Change Imperative for Whole System Reform* (Thousand Oaks, CA: Corwin, 2010), p. xiii.

22. Palmer, p. 12.

23. Cited in Palmer, p. 49.

# Index

# About the Author

**Sam Chaltain** began his career teaching high school English and history in New York City. Along the way, he co-directed a national network of schools, founded a leadership development program for K–12 principals, and ran an education policy think tank. Now he lives with his wife and two sons in Washington, D.C., where he writes about the state of teaching and learning in America, and how it can be strengthened.

The author or co-author of six books, Sam's writings have appeared in both magazines and newspapers, from *Forbes* to the *Washington Post*. He invites readers to email him directly at schaltain@gmail.com, or to connect with him via Twitter (@samchaltain), Facebook (schaltain), or his website, samchaltain.com.